The Historical-Critical Method

by
Edgar Krentz

Fortress Press

Philadelphia

Library of Congress Catalog Card Number 74-26345
ISBN 0-8006-0460-1

Printed in the United States of America   1-460

95   9   10

To Marion, the wife who helped;
John Tietjen, the president who defended;
and the Aid Association for Lutherans,
whose John Behnken fellowship
made the writing of this book financially possible

Editor's Foreword

The Historical-Critical Method serves as an introduction to the other works in the series *Guides to Biblical Scholarship*. Its purpose is to examine in general the foundations of what has come to be called the historical-critical investigation of the Bible. It traces the rise of this approach, examines its aims, methods, and presuppositions, and considers the implications of such work for theology.

The fundamental rule of biblical exegesis is that the interpreter must be obedient to the text itself; that is, he or she must allow the texts to determine their interpretation. Another way to put this is to say that understanding of a text must finally be "standing under," listening to, and hearing the text, and not one's own voice. Historical-critical scholarship furthers such interpretation, first by establishing a certain distance between interpreter and text. The biblical documents emerge in such analysis as words from another world, the history and culture of ancient Israel and the early church. They are, in a real sense, foreign documents. But second, historical-critical interpretation provides means to bridge the gap between interpreter and ancient text by relating them to a particular history, and by translating their foreign tongues. While the bridges built by historical-critical tools do not always lead as far as one might wish, they do point to real events and persons. Thus the historical-critical method helps to establish both distance from and intimacy with the texts, two factors which are essential to a dialogue in which both interpreter and text are given voices.

Important as they are, historical-critical tools are not the only ones essential for biblical interpretation. History and theology, for example, are not the same; few historical critics would deny the need for biblical theology as well. And other types of interpretation—such as structuralism and certain modes of literary analysis—are opening up other dimensions to the Bible.

The reader should understand that history, or historiography, and exegesis are by no means the same: history tries to reconstruct the past while exegesis attempts to unfold the meaning of texts. Yet the two are intimately related: on the one hand, any ancient text must be analyzed and interpreted before it can serve as a source for history, and on the other hand, texts from the past must be interpreted in terms of their historical meaning—what they said in and to their own times—as at least one step essential to their understanding. Thus no serious student of the Bible can ignore the issues treated in this volume.

Emory University
Atlanta, Georgia
Spring, 1975

GENE M. TUCKER

Contents

1
Introduction

The Bible, a treasure of all Christian churches, contains the irreplaceable primary documents of the Christian faith. The Bible is also a collection of ancient documents, written in strange and even exotic languages of other ages and cultures. Much in the Bible is foreign to urbanized Western civilization and requires explanation. The Bible is also the major source of information about the history of Israel in pre-Christian times and the origins of the Christian faith and the Christian church. Under all these aspects the Bible has been the source of information and doctrine, of faith and hope. Its interpretation has also been a battleground, for when men's hopes and most deeply held convictions are buttressed from the Bible, differences as to what the Bible says or how to read it provoke violent debate.

The controversy is as old as the Christian church itself; it has raged with peculiar force in three periods of change: the primitive church, the Reformation, and the period since the rise of modern criticism.[1] The first debate was between Christians and Jews over the christological interpretation of the Old Testament; the Reformation controversy raged over the single rather than a multiple sense of Scripture. Both these controversies were theological in nature. The crisis that came with the rise of historical criticism was different, for it had more philosophic and cultural overtones. It introduced into biblical interpretation a new method based on a secular understanding of history.

1. James Luther Mays, *Exegesis as a Theological Discipline* (Richmond, Va.: Union Theological Seminary, 1960), pp. 5–12. Gerhard Ebeling, *The Problem of Historicity in the Church and Its Proclamation*, trans. Grover Foley (Philadelphia: Fortress Press, 1967), p. 113 identifies the first crisis as the genesis of early catholic hermeneutics.

Although there are still those who raise questions, the method is now generally accepted, as recent pronouncements of various official church groups show. The Roman Catholic Church achieved slow but constant progress in this century toward approval of the method. The encyclical *Divino Afflante Spiritu* of Pope Pius XII (September 30, 1943) made the historical method not only permissible, but "a duty."[2] The *Instruction on the Historical Truth of the Gospels* (April 21, 1964) by the Pontifical Biblical Commission expressly confirmed the method and described the new aids to exegesis as source analysis, textual criticism, literary criticism, linguistic studies, and the method of form history.[3] The Ecumenical Study Conference held at Wadham College, Oxford (1949) produced a very similar listing of historical critical steps:

(1) the determination of the text; (2) the literary form of the passage; (3) the historical situation, the *Sitz im Leben;* (4) the meaning which the words had for the original author and hearer or reader; (5) the understanding of the passage in the light of its total context and the background out of which it emerged.[4]

The same steps were approved by the Commission on Theology and Church Relations of the Luthern Church–Missouri Synod in 1966.[5]

More private works show the same broad acceptance. The *Biblischer Kommentar–Altes Testament* uses the schema *Text, Form, Ort, Wort, Ziel,*[6] while G. E. Ladd virtually approves the same procedures within certain specific theological presuppositions.[7] Even so conservative a group as the *Kirchliche*

2. Latin text in *Acta Apostolicae Sedis*, 35 (1943): 297–325; a convenient English translation in *Rome and the Study of Scripture* (7th ed., St. Meinrad, Ind.: Grail Publications, 1964), pp. 80–127. The phrase *a duty* is used by Heinrich Zimmermann, *Neutestamentliche Methodenlehre* (4. Aufl., Stuttgart: Verlag Kath. Bibelwerk, 1974), p. 17, n. 1.
3. "Instructio de Historica Evangeliorum Veritate," *Catholic Biblical Quarterly*, 26 (1964): 299. It contains both Latin and English texts.
4. *Biblical Authority for Today*, ed. A. Richardson and W. Schweitzer (Philadelphia: Westminster Press, 1951), pp. 241–244.
5. In "A Lutheran Stance toward Contemporary Biblical Studies" (St. Louis, 1966).
6. Edited by Martin Noth (Neukirchen: Neukirchener Verlag, 1955—); Gottfried Adam, "Zur wissenschaftlichen Arbeitsweise," *Einführung in die exegetischen Methoden* (München: Chr. Kaiser Verlag, 1963), p. 80, urges the same steps.
7. *The New Testament and Criticism* (Grand Rapids, Mich.: Wm. B. Eerdmans, 1967).

Sammlung um Bibel und Bekenntnis gives general approval of historical criticism.[8] There is a general consensus about method; "... the battle for the acceptance of historical criticism as applied to the Bible has been won."[9] One can no longer distinguish liberal and conservative simply on the basis of exegetical method, although they do reach different conclusions.

The consensus was not reached without casualties. Many scholars, even in recent times, have paid the price of personal privation and suffering for their convictions. Historical criticism "has throughout its history almost always stood in the cross-fire of a generally less than joyful polemic from the side of unenlightened orthodox zealots. . . ."[10] That history is significant for the understanding of historical criticism today and will occupy us in chapter two.

All problems are not solved. The gap between scholarship and the church often is great. Many people still fear historical criticism in biblical studies. The results of critical scholarship have made the Bible a strange, unused, and even silent book.[11] Many Christians feel, as did Søren Kierkegaard, that the study of the Bible with commentary, dictionary, and the other tools of scholarship often is a way "of defending oneself against God's Word," not hearing it.[12] The feeling arises from fear, misunderstanding, and a nostalgia for the good old days when scholarship did not disturb the church. One counteracts such fear only by demonstrating that scholarship produces results that are responsible, useful, and beneficial for the proclamation of the church. Chapters three and four will indicate some of these useful results.

We cannot escape historical-critical study of the Bible. Its results appear in our daily newspapers, in books on the paperback rack in the stores, and in the curricula of our high schools

8. "The Braunschweig Theses on the Teaching and Mission of the Church," *Concordia Theological Monthly*, 37 (1966): 517.
9. R. P. C. Hanson, *Biblical Criticism* (Baltimore: Penguin Books, 1970), p. 3. It is now a truism in theological literature.
10. Josef Blank, "Die Interpretation der Bibel als theologisches Problem," *Schriftauslegung in Theorie und Praxis* (München: Kösel Verlag, 1969), p. 16.
11. James Smart, *The Strange Silence of the Bible in the Church* (Philadelphia: Westminster Press, 1970), pp. 15–31.
12. *For Self-Examination and Judge for Yourselves and Three Discourses, 1851*, trans. Walter Lowrie (Princeton: Princeton University Press, 1944), p. 56.

and colleges. Its presence raises the question of the nature of responsible and valid interpretation that reflects accurately the contents of biblical texts and tells us what happened in the past.

In recent years many questions have been raised about the adequacy of historical criticism by some of its committed users (Ferdinand Hahn, Peter Stuhlmacher, Martin Hengel). Others have tried to defend the method with an argument from Reformation theology. Still others have tried to define its validity without limiting theological thought to the Reformation (Trutz Rendtorff, Jürgen Moltmann). These most recent discussions will be summarized in chapter five.[13]

The introduction of historical criticism constituted "the most serious test that the church has had to face through nineteen centuries" about the nature of authority.[14] The method tends to freedom from authority and criticism of tradition. It treats biblical material in a different manner than theological thought had done for centuries, and in the process questions the validity of theological method. In the past the study of the Bible had been carried on in the church or in university faculties that prepared men for ordination. Today such study is more and more being done in university departments of religion that are in no way related to the church. The Bible is studied critically with the same methods used on all ancient literature.[15] Scholars must ask whether historical criticism, a legacy of historicism and its philosophic presuppositions, is adequate for the investigation of the Bible, a book that has shaped the beliefs and lives of millions of people for more than two millennia. Can it do justice to the inner meaning of religious literature?

In the following pages I will use recent literature on historiography by some representative contemporary historians as a means to understand and measure the goals, methods, and presuppositions of biblical scholarship. My aim is to describe what is being done, the limitations and the contributions of the

13. There will be no attempt to summarize the discussions of philosophy and theology concerning history. For that see Van A. Harvey, *The Historian and the Believer* (New York: Macmillan, 1966).
14. E. C. Blackman, *Biblical Interpretation* (Philadelphia: Westminster Press, 1959), p. 16.
15. See Paul S. Minear, "Gospel History: Celebration or Reconstruction," *Jesus and Man's Hope* (Pittsburgh: Pittsburgh Theological Seminary, 1971), II, 16.

method used, and the foci of current debate. I hope to give a kind of map of the current terrain, not an exploration of new territory. These pages are designed to orient college or seminary students so that they can intelligently participate in the evaluation of the predominant method of biblical interpretation in use today.

II

The Rise of Historical Criticism

Modern biblical scholars use a critical method, that is, a disciplined interrogation of their sources to secure a maximal amount of verified information. They seek the truth that is valuable for its own sake. The nature of the research distinguishes the method from the casual and almost accidental critical judgments in the premodern phase of biblical studies.

DOGMATIC CRITICISM

There were incidental but clear historical insights in the patristic era. Origen questioned the Pauline authorship of Hebrews on the basis of stylistic criteria (cf. Eusebius, *Hist. Eccl.* VI.25.11ff.). Dionysius of Alexandria argued from vocabulary and style that the author of the fourth Gospel could not have written the Apocalypse of John (Eusebius, *Hist. Eccl.* VII.25.1ff.), while Jerome (*De Viris Illus.* 1) reports that many doubted the Petrine authorship of 2 Peter on stylistic grounds.[1]

These insights were more dogmatically than historically motivated. Decisions on authorship were made in the process of determining canonicity, not to serve authentic historical interest. Marcion used historical improbabilities and moral

---

1. The evidence is gathered in Werner Georg Kümmel, *The New Testament: The History of the Investigation of Its Problems*, trans. S. McLean Gilmour and Howard C. Kee (Nashville and New York: Abingdon Press, 1972), pp. 15–18; hereafter cited as *NT*. The counterpart to this basic work for the Old Testament (Hans Joachim Kraus, *Geschichte der historisch-kritischen Erforschung des Alten Testaments* [2. Aufl., Neukirchen: Neukirchener Verlag, 1969]) has not yet been translated; see instead Herbert F. Hahn, *The Old Testament in Modern Research*, with a survey of recent literature by Horace D. Hummel (Philadelphia: Fortress Press, 1966).

laxity as canon criteria. To counter him the church used the theory of multiple senses based on Origen's idea of absolute inspiration. The attempt of the school of Antioch to use only the historical-grammatical sense failed. Ambrose, Hilary, Augustine, and the Western medieval commentators followed the East in rejecting the literal-grammatical sense by itself as a humiliation of Scripture. The concept of what was worthy of God triumphed over historical interests in a form of dogmatic criticism. Its classical formulation is the *Quod ubique, quod semper, quod ab omnibus creditum est* ("What has been believed everywhere, always, and by all"), ascribed to Vincent of Lerins. There was no truly free investigation in the patristic era.[2]

In the late medieval period Thomas Aquinas, John Gerson, and a few others urged a more strictly literal interpretation. Their exegesis became consciously more objective. This objectivity, according to Robert Grant, is "the beginning of the modern scientific study of the Scriptures. Reason is set up as an autonomous agent."[3] It is difficult, however, to trace a direct line of descent from late medieval theology to modern biblical studies.

THE FIRST RUSTLES OF CRITICISM: RENAISSANCE AND REFORMATION

The Renaissance brought a significant development: interest in antiquity. Manuscript collecting began, and shortly the printing press began to make copies available to scholarship.[4] After 1453, learned Byzantine expatriates brought the knowledge of Greek to Italy, where it was eagerly learned, promoted, and passed on to other countries. The study of Hebrew began, the outstanding figure being Johannes Reuchlin.[5] Thus

2. See Erich Dinkler, "Bibelautorität und Bibelkritik," *Signum Crucis* (Tübingen: J. C. B. Mohr, 1967), pp. 181–183; Josef Ernst, "Das hermeneutische Problem im Wandel der Auslegungsgeschichte," *Schriftauslegung* (München, Paderborn, Wien: Verlag Ferdinand Schöningh, 1972), pp. 19–25.

3. Robert Grant, *The Bible in the Church. A Short History of Interpretation* (New York: Macmillan, 1960), pp. 105–108; Ernst, "Das hermeneutische Problem," pp. 25–26.

4. The significance of printing cannot be overstressed. Aldus Manutius, the great Venetian printer (1494–1504), published a long series of texts, and he was only one of many. See John Edwin Sandys, *A History of Classical Scholarship* (Cambridge: at the University Press, 1903–1908), II, 25–34.

5. Max Brod, *Johannes Reuchlin und sein Kampf* (Stuttgart: W. Kohlhammer Verlag, 1965).

through its interest in sources the humanist Renaissance contributed philological tools to the interpretation of the Bible.[6]

Lorenzo Valla, a student of canon law, in 1440 demonstrated that the passage in the Decree of Gratian attesting the donation of Constantine (the gift of diadem and lands to Pope Sylvester I) was a forgery. His use of linguistic, legal, historical, and political arguments makes him one of the founders of historical criticism.[7] Ulrich von Hutten gave Valla's work great influence by printing it for the first time (1517) in Germany.

Humanists like Erasmus, Cajetan, and John Colet interpreted the Bible with the same methods they used on other ancient literature; they looked for the literal sense. They could not artificially stop this mode of thought at some boundary erected around the Scriptures. They gave the first impulse to the historical understanding of the Bible.[8] Erasmus coupled with this a demand for the use of reason in interpretation, and so made reason a criterion of interpretation.[9] Thus historical thought and the use of reason were legacies to the Reformation and later interpreters. The classical gymnasia promoted their approach and so influenced generations of biblical interpreters.

The Reformation marks a clear caesura in the history of exegesis. The Scriptures, not the tradition of the church, are to be the only judge in theology. Luther gave

. . . primacy to Scripture in all questions that are referred to the church fathers. This means that [Scripture] itself by itself is the most unequivocal, the most accessible, the most comprehensible authority, itself its own interpreter, attesting, judging, and illuminating all things. . . .[10]

6. Melanchthon applied the *ad fontes* cry to New Testament interpretation. We bring our spirits "to the sources"; *Corp. Ref.* VI. 23.

7. Sandys, *Classical Scholarship*, II, 67; Grant, *The Bible in the Church*, p. 118.

8. Ernst, "Das hermeneutische Problem," pp. 29–30; Josef Schreiner, "Zur Geschichte der alttestamentlichen Exegese: Epochen, Ziele, Wege," *Einführung in die Methoden der biblischen Exegese*, ed. Josef Schreiner (Tyrolia: Echter Verlag, 1971), p. 13.

9. Luther argued strongly against Erasmus (Dinkler, "Bibelautorität," pp. 186–188). Although Trent condemned Cajetan's views, and Erasmus bowed to the church, the influence of humanism continued through Protestant humanists (Sandys, *Classical Scholarship*, II, 258).

10. *Assertio omnium articulum M. Lutheri per Bullam Leonis X. novissimam damnatorum* (1519, WA, VII, 97), as translated in Kümmel, *NT*, p. 22. See F. Beisser, *Claritas Scripturae bei M. Luther* (Göttingen: Vandenhoeck & Ruprecht, 1966).

Luther affirmed that the Bible in its literal sense was clear and open to all. This literal sense was the place where the Holy Spirit worked, not in the tradition of the Roman Church or the immediate experience of the Enthusiasts.[11] Luther used all the means that the humanists had developed to discover this literal sense: Hebrew and Greek philology, the Erasmus Greek Testament, and the historical background of a book.[12] Yet he insisted that the Holy Spirit was necessary for a proper interpretation.

Luther's affirmation of scriptural clarity brought two problems in its train. (1) How does one choose between different interpretations that claim to be based on the literal sense? Erasmus had answered, by reason. Luther elected instead to interpret the entire Scripture from its central point, Christ. "Take Christ from the Scriptures! What else is there to be found in them?"[13] Where passages are unclear (and there are such), the interpreter's task is to relate them to this Gospel. Melanchthon expressed the same view in *Apology of the Augsburg Confession* IV. (2) Luther applied the same principle to the problem of the canon. Some books fall short of a proper proclamation of the Gospel. James mentions Jesus only twice. Hebrews regards repentance after a fall from baptismal faith impossible (6:4–6; 10:26–31). Luther's evangelical canon for the canon is *"Was Christum treibet"* ("What urges Christ") in his "Preface" to the New Testament (1522) and the prefaces to the individual books. James, Jude, Hebrews, and the Apocalypse fall short of the standard; John, Romans, Galatians, and 1 Peter form the core and are superior to other books.[14] Some

11. Albrecht Oepke, *Geschichtliche und übergeschichtliche Schriftauslegung* (2. Aufl., Gütersloh: C. Bertelsmann, 1947), pp. 9–10.

12. See his "Preface to the Book of Isaiah," *Luther's Works* (Philadelphia: Fortress Press, 1960), 35. See Kümmel, *NT*, pp. 22–23 on the literal sense in Luther (with bibliography).

13. *De servo arbitrio*, WA, XVIII, 606. On Christ as the *punctum mathematicum* see A. E. Buchrucker, "Die regula atque norma in der Theologie Luthers," *Neue Zeitschrift für systematische Theologie*, 10 (1968): 131–169; Jaroslav Pelikan, *Luther the Expositor* (St. Louis: Concordia Publishing House, 1959). Luther read the Old Testament christologically also; see H. Bornkamm, *Luther and the Old Testament*, trans. Victor I. Gruhn (Philadelphia: Fortress Press, 1969).

14. The Prefaces are printed in *Luther's Works* (Philadelphia: Fortress Press, 1960), 35; relevant excerpts in Kümmel, *NT*, pp. 24–26. On their significance see W. G. Kümmel, "The Continuing Significance of Luther's Prefaces to the New Testament," *Concordia Theological Monthly*, 37 (1966): 573–581; Maurice E. Schild, *Abendländische Bibelvorreden bis zur Lutherbibel* (Gütersloh: Gerd Mohn, 1970), pp. 166–264. Luther also used literary and historical arguments in his prefaces.

feel that Luther here introduced a subjective element into interpretation. Others invoke this insight of Luther's as the justification for present-day content criticism (*Sachkritik*).

Zwingli and Calvin also stressed the Bible as the single authority in the church, but did not follow Luther's christological approach. Calvin derived the Bible's authority from the theologoumenon that God himself is the speaker in the Bible. His position led to a more rigid view of the literal sense and its application.[15] Matthias Flacius Illyricus was close in spirit to Calvin. His *Clavis Scripturae Sacrae* (1567), the first hermeneutics text, is a landmark in the history of exegesis. Flacius demanded the discovery of the literal sense, i.e., the "sense that it conveyed to its original readers."[16] Apparent contradictions can be resolved if one observes carefully the Bible's purpose (*scopus*) and uses the *analogia fidei* as a guide. Luther's Gospel center is absent here. Yet Flacius' basic principles point to a truly historical interpretation.

The Reformers freed the Scriptures to exercise a critical function in the church. They found a criterion of interpretation in the literal sense. One decides between variant interpretations by looking at the intention of the texts, understood either as the Gospel (Luther) or the *analogia fidei* (the analogy of faith, Flacius). In Luther *Sachkritik* enters for the first time. Luther also argued that the work of the Holy Spirit by the Word would create the proper understanding. Thus one form of the hermeneutical circle is introduced into exegesis; the question of the relation of faith and historical method raised then is still discussed today.[17]

THE RISE OF METHODICAL DOUBT

In the seventeenth century science, history, and philosophy became autonomous disciplines, freed from both biblical authority and the traditional masters in their fields (Aristotle, Ptolemy, etc.). The result, a new method of achieving knowl-

15. *Inst.* I. VII, as cited in Grant, *The Bible in the Church*, pp. 113–114.
16. The phrase is Kümmel's, based on quotations from the *Clavis* (*NT*, pp. 28–29). G. Ebeling, "Hermeneutik," *Die Religion in der Geschichte und Gegenwart* (3. Aufl. Tübingen: Mohr, 1959), III, 252 stresses the significance of the *Clavis*.
17. Karl Lehmann, "Der hermeneutische Horizont der historisch kritischen Exegese," *Einführung* (above, note 8), pp. 43–44; Ernst, "Das hermeneutische Problem," p. 27.

edge, affected biblical interpretation. The key figures were not theologians, but men who were regarded by the church "only as impertinent, derogatory, and blasphemous outsiders."[18] Klaus Scholder recently studied the encroachment of secular knowledge on biblical authority in this century. His outstanding study will be our major guide.[19]

At the beginning of the seventeenth century the Bible was the universal authority in all fields of knowledge, but by the end of the century that authority was eroded. In 1543 Andreas Osiander challenged biblical authority by publishing Copernicus' *De Revolutionibus Orbium Coelestium* with his own preface. He pointed out that the heliocentric view was only a theory, to be judged by how adequately it accounted for celestial phenomena. The theoretical character of his work was enough to keep opposition to a minimum.[20] But Copernicus' theory was given much higher probability by Johannes Kepler's mathematical proofs in the seventeenth century. Kepler reconciled his views with the Bible by proposing a theory of accommodation in biblical language, thus preserving the Bible from error. "In truth the sacred writings speak about everyday things (in which they were not designed to give man instruction) in human fashion, as things are perceived by men. . . ." (*Opera*, III, 153). Kepler concludes that, in science, reason based on the evidence of observation is stronger than the fathers' opinions (Scholder, pp. 66–71). The results of science should be used to understand the Bible.[21] A new world view and a new inductive science that concerned itself with this world, not with Aristotle's unseen teleological mover, were born. Science worked independently of the Bible—and in that way the Bible's authority was diminished.

18. Kendrick Grobel, "Biblical Criticism," *The Interpreter's Dictionary of the Bible* (New York, Nashville: Abingdon Press, 1962), I, 409. Grobel refers to Grotius, Hobbes, Spinoza, and Astruc.

19. Klaus Scholder, *Ursprünge und Probleme der Bibelkritik im 17. Jahrhundert. Ein Beitrag zur Entstehung der hist. krit. Theologie* (München: Chr. Kaiser Verlag, 1966). Alan Richardson, *The Bible in the Age of Science* (London: SCM Press, 1961), pp. 9–31 has a useful short discussion.

20. Scholder, *Ursprünge*, pp. 60–65. Melanchthon opposed Copernicus by arguing that the Bible necessitated a geocentric view (Scholder, pp. 58–59).

21. Galileo comes to similar conclusions (Scholder, *Ursprünge*, pp. 72–74). Both men were oppressed for their beliefs; see Richardson, *The Bible in the Age of Science*, pp. 16–18, 21-22.

The study of history followed a similar path. The Bible had been *the* authority for world chronology and geography.[22] Now new knowledge from new sources revealed the limitations of the historical and chronological data in the Bible. Jean Bodin's demand that reason be used for the writing of history (Scholder, p. 91) and Joachim Vadian's argument for observation in writing geography (Scholder, p. 96) weakened the Bible's authority in historical study.

The *facit* was drawn with the publication of Isaac de La Peyrère's *Prae-Adamiten* in 1655, an attempt to reconcile the new knowledge with the Bible. He argued that a combination of the geographical and chronological data with a careful exegesis of Rom. 5:12–14 compelled the conclusion that Adam was not the first man, but only the progenitor of the Israelites. La Peyrère pointed to gaps and contradictions in the biblical material and used the results of history and empirical science to question the traditional exegesis. It had erred, he said, in understanding a specific, local statement as a general truth about all history (Scholder, pp. 98–102).

The Pre-Adamite controversy followed, producing strong reaction from all branches of Western Christendom. The flood of scholarly response quite easily refuted the book exegetically (Scholder, p. 103), but did not face the basic question: how is the new knowledge to be reconciled with biblical authority? Orthodoxy demanded instead a *sacrificium intellectus* in the face of the Bible's statements. After that only two responses were possible: either one must recognize two independent truths (which satisfied no one), or a struggle for supremacy must result. Orthodoxy's best reaction would have been a better and more comprehensive theory to account for the new data. The failure to provide that alternative ". . . . cut the last bonds that were still restraining criticism. That was finally the result of the Orthodox polemic" (Scholder, p. 104). Orthodoxy gave criticism a freedom from dialogue, for the outsiders felt there was no real conversational partner in the church and so disregarded her.

Meanwhile in the Abbey de Saint-Germaine des Prés outside of Paris Jean Mabillon, a Benedictine monk, was quietly work-

22. Melanchthon argues that since the Bible was older, more complete, and more precise than all other sources, all historical reconstruction should begin from it. See his introduction to the *Chronicon* of Carion, *Corp. Ref.*, XII, 711–712, cited by Scholder, *Ursprünge*, pp. 82–83. Luther agreed, using Daniel as his basic scheme.

ing on the first volume of the *Acta Sanctorum* (1668), "a historic work of the highest order, which was characterized throughout by a never-failing love of truth." Mabillon worked out the means for determining the date and authenticity of ancient documents, a cornerstone in historical method.[23]

Changes in philosophy were equally striking and more significant.[24] In 1637 René Descartes's *Discours de la Méthode* raised doubt to a universally valid principle and changed philosophic, scientific, and historical method down to the present day. He used three basic principles: (1) Man, as thinking subject, is the center of philosophical inquiry. *Cogito, ergo sum.* (2) Nothing is accepted as true simply because it is in the tradition; doubt everything except what is so evident to one's own thought that there is no basis for doubt. (3) Reason is the sole criterion of truth. Bloch (p. 84) emphasizes that Cartesian doubt is positive: one doubts to arrive at new certainties. Descartes personally kept the mysteries of faith removed from the realm of reason, but his followers insisted that they answer the question of truth at the bar of reason. (Scholder, pp. 132–135). Orthodoxy responded to Descartes as it had to La Peyrère: dogmatically. One must make reason captive to Scripture, for fallen reason is no guide to knowledge (Scholder, pp. 140–142).

Descartes's followers split into two groups. A moderate wing held that there were two kinds of truth, separate but not contradictory. Reason can and must think critically in natural matters. The Scriptures are authoritative only within their own *scopus*, the transmission of matters of faith. This separation of Scripture and reason was an attempt to save the truth of Scripture and offered a mode of rapprochement between theology and philosophy (Scholder, pp. 146–158).

But it was not to be. The more radical Cartesians captured the intellectual stage with their refusal to separate truth. Truth

23. Sandys, *Classical Scholarship*, II, 295. Marc Bloch, *The Historian's Craft* (Manchester: Manchester University Press, 1954), p. 81, calls the year of the publication of Mabillon's *De Re Diplomatica* (1681) "a great one in the history of the human mind," for this work established the criticism of documents. In Holland Perizonius anticipated in a little masterpiece the later critical history of early Rome. However, his work had little immediate effect (Sandys, II, 330–331).

24. Hugo Grotius (a student of international law) and Thomas Hobbes argued that the Bible must be read like any other book, and that biblical books' date and authorship must be determined from internal evidence only. See Grobel, "Biblical Criticism," p. 409; Grant, *The Bible in the Church*, p. 124.

is one and rational, so religion must also be rational or it is not true. Reason was made the norm over religion and the Scriptures. The Thirty Years' War showed what destruction could come from religious convictions. Baruch Spinoza's *Tractatus Theologico-Politicus* (1670), written in the years after that war, used reason as a better guide to men's minds. Spinoza gathered the scholarly research of the previous century and used it in a basic critique of religion. "Truth cannot contradict truth." Therefore Scripture, often hard to understand, must be subject to and agree with reason. Reason itself is absolutely unfettered by religious sanctions, for philosophy has a different basis and goal from those of theology. Philosophy, based on nature, therefore works out of the common notions and ideas of man to seek truth. Theology, based on history and discourse, works out of revelation to secure obedience and piety. The spheres do not conflict (Grant, p. 126; Scholder, pp. 166–167).

Spinoza discusses biblical interpretation to discredit the appearance of supernatural authority. Miracles in the Bible are the result of the Jewish custom of referring everything to God in disregard of secondary causes.[25] Revelation as such does not happen. Consistently, in chapter seven of the *Tractatus* Spinoza's rules for biblical interpretation state that the Bible is to be studied like any other book with a clear, rational, and essentially untheological method.[26]

Spinoza lived in the springtime of rationalism, when the uncertainties of inferior religion were to disappear before superior reason. Self-confident reason would not allow any authority outside of itself to endure. The Bible is either rational or its authority must be destroyed. The tools of destruction were at hand: the demonstration by reason that the Bible's stories were fictions, its historical reliability low, and its theological statements surpassed by the discoveries of reason. Criticism of the Bible became negative and destructive (Scholder, pp. 169–170).

25. "I must . . . premise that the Jews never make any mention or account of secondary or particular causes, but in a spirit of religion, piety, and what is commonly called godliness, refer all things directly to the Deity. . . . Hence we must not suppose that everything is prophecy or revelation which is described in Scripture as told by God to anyone." *Tract.*, chap. I, translated in Grant, *The Bible in the Church*, p. 126.
26. Grant, *The Bible in the Church*, summarizes the rules (pp. 127–128), Grobel, "Biblical Criticism," the results (pp. 409–410).

In this century the church was on the defensive, its theologians fighting a rear guard action. Those who tried to engage in the debate with reason were denounced. When Joachim Stegman, a Socinian, raised the question of the relation of reason to doctrine and Scripture, the church condemned him by asserting that Scripture is the *principium cognoscendi*, the principle of knowledge. Because the church did not enter the debate, the place of reason in theology remained unclear.

In the last quarter of the century the French Oratorian priest Richard Simon published a series of books in which he applied critical method to the Bible (1678 ff.). With these he became the direct founder of the historical-critical study of the Bible. His aim was apologetic, not historical, to show that the Protestant *sola scriptura* principle, when carried to its logical conclusion, makes confidence in the Bible impossible. The literal sense interpreted by the true laws of criticism produces uncertainty, unless it is accompanied by tradition as guide. In arguing that Moses could not have written the entire Pentateuch, that some biblical books reflect a long period of compilation, and that the textual tradition is uncertain, Simon used the evident and the rational as criteria, i.e., he practiced criticism of the Bible. He was expelled from the Oratorians in 1678 and his writings were placed on the *Index*.[27]

The last great dogmatic systems in Protestantism were written in the seventeenth century (John Gerhard, *Loci Communes Theologici*, 9 vol., 1610–1622; Abraham Calov, *Systema Locorum Theologicorum*, 12 vol., 1655–1672, etc.). They were important, yet futile, attempts to secure the Scriptures as Word of God. Their earnestness and integrity must be respected, yet these systems finally were inadequate because they were written out of fear of change, fear of losing the basis for the certainty of faith, and fear of posing questions in the area of authority. It is ironic that the inability of the writers to leave the categories of their dogmatic position did more to prepare the way for the triumph of radical Cartesianism than they ever dreamed. Orthodoxy made the position of rationalism seem more attractive than it really was. In defending the faith it helped to undermine it—all unaware![28]

27. Texts in Kümmel, *NT*, pp. 40–46. See also Reinhart Koselleck, *Kritik und Krise* (Suhrkamp Taschenbuch, 1973), pp. 87–88.
28. Scholder, *Ursprünge* pp. 142–144; Hans Grass, "Historisch-kritische

This century saw the first rules of criticism (Mabillon), the introduction of methodological doubt (Descartes), the restriction of biblical authority by science and history, and the growing triumph of reason over revelation. The Scriptures were more and more treated like ordinary historical documents. The process of objectification had begun.

THE ADVENT OF HISTORICAL CRITICISM: THE ENLIGHTENMENT

Reason's triumph over revelation came to full flower after Spinoza. In England Deism reigned, beginning with John Locke's *Essay on Human Understanding* (1690) and *The Reasonableness of Christianity as Delivered in the Scriptures* (1695). Locke argued that "reason is natural revelation." God communicates to man through his natural powers new discoveries which reason validates by offering proofs. Remove reason and you remove revelation.[29] The eighteenth-century Deists treated the Bible with freedom when it did not, in their lights, accord with reason. For example, they argued that Isaiah was composite, the Gospels contradictory, and the apostles often unreliable. More able men (Berkeley, Butler, Addison, Pope, Swift, Bentley, Law, etc.) defeated them in the controversies they raised, but the victory left Scripture's authority in a "much weakened position." The Bible was now discussed, attacked, and defended like a "common, man-made philosophy," for the opponents of the Deists also used the power of reason in defending the Bible (Neil, pp. 243-244). Thus Deism strengthened tendencies, latent in earlier interpretation, toward a more truly historical approach (Kümmel, p. 58). Deism, strongest from 1700 to 1750, issued at the end of the century in David Hume's skepticism about God and providence, in Edward Gibbon's antisupernaturalism, and in Tom Paine's crude but understandable popularization in the *Age of Reason* (1795), for which Paine's publishers were fined and sent to prison. Deism might have ruled longer but for the horror of the French Revolution, credited by many English-

Forschung und Dogmatik," *Theologie und Kritik* (Göttingen: Vandenhoeck & Ruprecht, 1969), pp. 9-10.
29. Locke, *Essay on Human Understanding*, IV. 19, §4, as cited by W. Neil, "The Criticism and Theological Use of the Bible," *The Cambridge History of the Bible*, vol. III: *The West from the Reformation to the Present Day* (Cambridge: at the University Press, 1963), p. 240; Norman Sikes, "The Religion of Protestants," ibid., pp. 195-197.

men to the criticism practiced by French rationalism (Neil, pp. 249–254).

In France imported English Deism mixed with seventeenth-century rationalism to give birth to the Enlightenment. Pierre Bayle provided an arsenal of argumentation in his *Dictionnaire historique et critique* (1695) for Voltaire, Rousseau, and Diderot to support Bayle's view that criticism has the right to make all areas of human thought its realm. Reason, the advocate for both pro and con, is the only instrument adequate to discover truth. All binding authorities (political, social, and religious) must fall before it; they have no common ground with reason (Koselleck, pp. 88–92). Bayle set the tone for an anti-church polemic that characterized French intellectual life throughout the century and gave the term *criticism* its abiding negative connotation.

The German *Aufklärung* (Enlightenment) did not evoke such strong antipathy to theology. The *Aufklärung* sought the eternal truths concealed in biblical history by purifying it of all inadequate forms. The *Aufklärung* shared with classical orthodoxy the conviction that there was one eternal, universally valid, internally consistent *pura doctrina sacra*. To that degree it stands in the Reformation tradition. However, it used reason, not Scripture or revelation, to find this doctrine.[30] Holy Scripture contains truth, but general truth that man would recognize in any case, for all truth is rational, and what is rational is capable of proof.

Lessing formulated the famous sentence that implies the limits of history and the function of historical study: "The contingent truths of history can never become the proof of the necessary truths of reason."[31] Historical revelation is a useful shortcut to the truth reason could find by itself. Historical investigation is the way to study revelation, and therefore is a useful tool. But its goal is nonhistorical, to find the highest stage of human thought, the rational and timeless truth toward which history and religion have been progressing (Ernst, p. 34). History is studied to remove it in favor of nonhistorical truth.

30. Ulrich Wilckens, "Über die Bedeutung historischer Kritik in der modernen Bibelexegese," *Was heisst Auslegung der Heiligen Schrift?* (Regensburg: Friedrich Pustet, 1966), pp. 95–96.
31. "Über den Beweis des Geistes und der Kräfte," (Rilla ed., VIII, p. 12), as cited by Friedrich Mildenberger, *Theologie für die Zeit* (Stuttgart: Calwer Verlag, 1969), p. 20.

In the eighteenth century historical criticism developed and made its way into the church. The critical text of the New Testament received a firm foundation. John Mill's edition (1707) made the first extensive set of variants available. Johann Albrecht Bengel (1734) classified them and formulated basic rules for evaluating them, while Johann Jakob Wettstein (1751–52) devised the modern notation system for listing the manuscripts (Kümmel, pp. 47–50). Earlier, the English classicist Richard Bentley, a cantankerous genius, had formulated the proper principles for a critical Greek Testament (1716 and 1720), but never produced an edition.[32] Later Johann Salamo Semler distinguished the earlier and later texts (Kümmel, pp. 66–67) and Johann Jakob Griesbach (1774–1775) printed the first reconstructed Greek text (not the textus receptus), thereby demonstrating the fitness of Bentley's comment, *nobis et ratio et res ipsa centum codicibus potiores sunt* ("Reason and the subject matter are in our opinion more powerful than a hundred codices," Horace edition of 1711, Sandys, II, 406). Bentley and Griesbach provided a firm basis for further work.

Theologians slowly arrived at a more historical interpretation of the Bible. In 1728 Jean Alphonse Turretinus of Geneva urged interpreting the Bible like other books: "One must put oneself into the times and into the surroundings in which [biblical authors] wrote, and one must see what [concepts] could arise in the souls of those who lived at that time."[33] Some twenty years later Wettstein demanded that the interpreter set himself "in the place of those to whom [the books] were first delivered by the Apostles as a legacy" (Kümmel, p. 50). A decade further on Johann August Ernesti in his *Institutio Interpretis Novi Testamenti* (1761) separated the Old and New Testaments in exegetical treatment. He applied the philological-historical method he had used with success earlier in editing classical texts to the New Testament, and thus became the "father of the profane scientific interpretation" of the Bible.[34]

Johann Salamo Semler rather than Ernesti is usually

32. Stephen Neill, *The Interpretation of the New Testament 1861–1961* (London: Oxford, 1966), p. 65.
33. *Concerning the Methods of Interpreting the Holy Scriptures*, cited in Kümmel, *NT*, p. 59; Wilckens, *Was heisst Auslegung*, pp. 93–94.
34. So Franz Lau, *Neue Deutsche Biographie* (Berlin: Duncker & Humbolt, 1959), IV, 605.

regarded as the father of historical-critical theology, since Ernesti denied the possibility of inspired Scripture ever erring.[35] Semler's major *opus*, a four-volume study on the free investigation of the canon (1771–1775), called for a purely historical-philological interpretation of the Bible, in the light of the circumstances surrounding the origin of the various books, without any concern for edification (Ebeling, col. 254). He distinguished the Scriptures and the Word of God, since some books belong in the Bible through historical decisions of past ages, but do not make wise unto salvation. For him much of the Old Testament lost all but historical relevance. Inspiration had given way to impartial history (Kümmel, pp. 62–69; Schreiner, p. 14). K. A. G. Keil drew the logical conclusion when he described the task of historical-grammatical interpretation as thinking an author's thoughts after him without passing value judgments on their historicity or truth. The exegete should only establish facts. The standard for subsequent commentaries was formulated (Ernst, p. 31; Kümmel, pp. 108–109).

This historical interest had profound effects. Great interest was aroused in the origins of documents by the attempt of Jean Astruc, a professor of medicine, to separate sources in the Pentateuch. He identified four in his *Conjectures on the Reminiscences which Moses Appears to Have Used in Composing the Book of Genesis* (1753), partly on the basis of the variation in use of divine names.[36] The four-source theory was on its way. The Synoptic Problem was posed, and Griesbach provided a basic tool in the first Greek synopsis (the printing of the Synoptics in parallel columns). Many theories were presented by a host of scholars (Lessing, Griesbach, Eichhorn, Herder, Schleiermacher). The theories were not convincing, but a fundamental historical problem had been recognized.[37]

A new discipline was born, Introduction to the Old/New Testament. The fourth edition of J. D. Michaelis's *Introduction to the New Testament* (1788) complied with Semler's require-

---

35. G. Hornig, *Die Anfänge der historisch-kritischen Theologie* (Göttingen: Vandenhoeck & Ruprecht, 1961).

36. Alexander Geddes followed his lead in the first volume of a new translation in 1792 (Grobel, "Biblical Criticism," pp. 410–411; Neil, "The Criticism and Theological Use of the Bible," pp. 270–272).

37. See Kümmel, *NT*, pp. 74–84, for an overview of the theories. Schleiermacher (1807) and Eichhorn (1812) raised the problem of the authenticity of the Pastorals.

ments for historical work and was "a comprehensive discussion of the historical problems of the New Testament and its individual books" (Kümmel, p. 69). The first edition (1750) was still under the influence of Simon. Michaelis read the New Testament on its own terms without dogmatic presuppositions and allowed for the possibility of contradictions. For him apostolic authorship guaranteed inspiration; nonapostolic books were neither inspired nor canonical. This rather unhappy solution to the question whether the authority of New Testament books depends on apostolic authorship has burdened theology ever since.[38] J. G. Eichhorn wrote the first modern *Einleitung in das Alte Testament* (3 vol., 1780–1783). Grobel (p. 411) summarized its significance:

Eichhorn's enduring merit is that he, more than any other, naturalized within Protestant theological investigation the humanist insight that the OT, like any other literature, may and must be fully and freely scrutinized, free from tradition, dogma, and institutional authority.

Eichhorn and Michaelis set the pattern that is still in use today.

A new interest in the life of Jesus and the relation of his teaching to that of the apostles arose. The publication of the *Fragmente eines Ungenannten* [H. S. Reimarus] by G. E. Lessing, the Wolfenbüttel librarian, opened the question dramatically. Reimarus used doubt with rationalist presuppositions as the instrument of historical work. His conclusions that Jesus was a deluded eschatological visionary, that miracles should be explained as natural phenomena, and that the disciples stole the body of the crucified Jesus were reached by an arbitrary historical criticism. Semler, for example, objected to the lack of source analysis and argued fervently against Reimarus's conclusions.[39] Reimarus raised the problems that occupy New Testament scholarship to the present: Jesus as eschatological preacher, the messianic secret, the passion predictions

38. So Neill, *Interpretation*, pp. 5–6. Herbert Marsh's translation into English (1793–1801) caused little stir in England.
39. Semler argued more effectively than Pastor Goetze of Hamburg, whose name is usually mentioned. See Grobel, "Biblical Criticism," p. 412; Wilckens, *Was heisst Auslegung*, pp. 97–99; Kümmel, *NT*, pp. 89–90. The classic survey of the lives of Jesus is that of Albert Schweitzer, *The Quest of the Historical Jesus*, trans. W. Montgomery (New York: Macmillan, 1948), with later reprints.

and the surprise of the disciples at the resurrection, miracles, "creative additions," the differences between John and the Synoptics, etc. The violent reaction led to many lives of Jesus, among which that by Karl Hase (1829) has been called "the first account of Jesus that at essential points is historical."[40]

Johann Philipp Gabler called for a truly historical New Testament theology, and set forth the difference between dogmatic and biblical theology in his inaugural address of 1787.

Gabler also introduced the concept of myth into New Testament studies. He followed, as exegesis often has, the lead of classical philology. Christian Gottlob Heyne had founded the scientific study of mythology. He held that myths sum up the beliefs and ideas of primitive people prior to their learning the art of writing.[41] Eichhorn applied the idea to New Testament angelology, and then Georg Lorenz Bauer laid out a series of rules for recognizing myth (in his *Hermeneutics*, 1799).[42] Bauer regarded the identification of myth as part of the task of determining the original sense of the words (and thus followed Reformation insights). Myth was removed to lay bare the truth it contains. Bauer demanded a new kind of *Sachkritik*, different from that of Luther. Now the study of the origins and literary expression of an idea was part of the practice of historical criticism.[43]

The rationalist Enlightenment radicalized the claim of reason and history; as a result it placed the claims of religion outside the realm of reason. In this division Orthodox theology lost its foundations in history. The cleft between reason and history triumphed among the learned—including the theologians—and removed the basis of orthodoxy's epistemology.[44]

---

40. Kümmel, *NT*, pp. 90–95, quote from p. 93.
41. Sandys, *Classical Scholarship*, III, 42. Heyne, an outstanding innovator in classical philology, inaugurated courses in archaeology (1767) and introduced into philological methods (!) the study of *realia* as opposed to the study of words. He anticipated the broad interest of nineteenth-century historians.
42. The rules are given in Kümmel, *NT*, p. 112, and Ernst, "Das hermeneutische Problem," p. 32.
43. W. G. Kümmel, "Das Erbe des 19. Jahrhunderts für die neutestamentliche Wissenschaft von heute," *Heilsgeschehen und Geschichte* (Marburg: Elwert, 1965), p. 368. A shortened version in *Das Neue Testament im 20. Jahrhundert. Ein Forschungsbericht* (Stuttgart: Verlag Kath. Bibelwerk, 1970), pp. 8–27. Cited here as *Erbe* according to the longer form.
44. Gerhard Ebeling, *The Problem of Historicity*, trans. Grover Foley (Philadelphia: Fortress Press, 1967), pp. 29–30.

Few Orthodox scholars learned historical method without taking over rationalist antisupernaturalism.

The historical thought of the Enlightenment was more philosophical than historical. It recognized the time-conditioned, historical character of the Bible (a major contribution) only to remove it through the application of common sense to historical materials (Lehmann, pp. 44–46; Neil, p. 239). History was used in the service of the religion of nature (reason) only "to point a moral or adorn a tale." The great achievement and literary excellence of Edward Gibbon's *Decline and Fall* should not blind us to the fact that it was history told to support an antisupernaturalist position (Richardson, pp. 41–44).

Nevertheless, the impulses for true historical study—not to support a philosophical position, but to understand the past—were present. The historical character of all revelation and doctrine was now clear. Herder was one of the first to point, even if unclearly, to the historicity of man and his entire world. He stressed that all historical phenomena are unique and singular, and so removed from analogical criticism.[45] The stage was set for the flowering of true historical interest and method.

HISTORICAL METHOD SET FREE: 1820–1920

An intellectual and social revolution changed all thought in the nineteenth century. Geology offered proof for the great antiquity of man, while evolutionary development was a commonplace by the end of the century. The fiery debate between science and theology soon died down, although the afterglow survives to the present. An economic and social revolution changed population and work patterns into those of the modern world. The optimistic spirit of growth and progress waltzed through the mental halls of Western civilization (Richardson, pp. 47–49).

The development of historical method can be documented in a series of works published within two decades. With Barthold Georg Niebuhr's *Römische Geschichte* (1811–1812) historical criticism came of age. Niebuhr used criticism to separate poetry and falsehood from truth in the sources from ancient Rome. He sought "at a minimum to discover with probability the web of events (*Zusammenhang*) and [to reconstruct] a

45. Klaus Scholder, "Herder und die Anfänge der historischen Theologie," *Evangelische Theologie*, 22 (1962): 425–440.

more believable narrative in place of the one he sacrificed to his convictions."[46] Criticism was used positively, to write the history of early Rome. Niebuhr asked two questions consistently and clearly: "What is the evidence?" and "What is the value of the evidence?" He began the process of making the sources say far more than they intended by uncovering their *Tendenz* (bias). The result was a new, exciting, and convincing picture of the origins of Rome—and a new historical tool. Niebuhr's influence was immense.

In 1824 Leopold von Ranke's *Geschichte der romanischen und germanischen Völker,* vol. I, appeared. In the preface von Ranke expressed his purpose as simply telling what really happened.[47] He was convinced that the criticism of the sources would give the purest, most objective knowledge (Kupisch, pp. 37–38). Yet he did not restrict himself to collecting facts (although he assembled vast numbers of them). History is unified; although he can only know history in its empirical form, the historian must seek that unity. A pious, believing Christian throughout his life (Kupisch, p. 12), von Ranke believed that God acted in history, but the historian cannot demonstrate his presence. Every moment in history is equally distant from this God. A theory of progress becomes unnecessary.[48]

Nine years later the twenty-five-year-old Johann Gustav Droysen published *Alexander the Great,* the first of his many historical works. Droysen called attention to the post-classical Greek world, whose syncretism was a stage on the road to

46. *Römische Geschichte,* I (1811), Introduction, p. x, as cited in Klaus Scholder, "Ferdinand Christian Baur als Historiker," *Evangelische Theologie,* 21 (1961): 438; see also Karl Christ, *Von Gibbon zu Restoftzeff* (Darmstadt: Wissenschaftliche Buchgesellschaft, 1972), and Karl Kupisch, *Der Hieroglyphe Gottes. Grosse Historiker der bürgerlichen Epoche von Ranke bis Meinecke* (München: Chr. Kaiser Verlag, 1967).
47. ". . . er will bloss zeigen, wie es eigentlich gewesen ist." Cited by Scholder, *Baur,* p. 440, from von Ranke's collected works, vol. 33/34, p. vii. Von Ranke came to source criticism via Niebuhr and became a master of it, setting the standard for subsequent historians. Kupisch, *Der Hieroglyphe Gottes,* pp. 15–16.
48. Scholder, *Baur,* p. 442; Kupisch, *Der Hieroglyphe Gottes,* pp. 34–35; Jürgen Moltmann, "Exegese und Eschatologie der Geschichte," *Perspektiven der Theologie* (München: Chr. Kaiser Verlag, 1968), p. 64. William von Humboldt held that historical criticism should lead to the discovery of the (pantheistic) truth that is in history. Scholder, *Baur,* pp. 438–439. Scholder argues sharply that James M. Robinson's description of historical positivism as interested only in the collection of facts is falsely derived from a narrow interest in *Leben Jesu* research, p. 439, note 15.

Christianity. He followed his teacher August Boeckh in using nonintentional sources (e.g, coins and inscriptions) for the writing of history. He was very critical of von Ranke's source criticism, and held that the historian is to seek the higher ethical progress visible in history.

This romantic school of history was strongly motivated by the concept of some divine or sensible idea moving through all history, whether it was Hegel's World Spirit, Humboldt's pantheistic truth, von Ranke's governing God, or Droysen's ethical progress. After 1850 historical inquiry grew more imminentist; historians were content to describe things as they had been. Eduard Meyer represents this position well. Meyer held that the historian is simply to portray individual happenings, not to find that history conforms to laws or general ideas. His task is to investigate what is, or at least once was, effective, and then to portray it in its infinite variety (Christ, pp. 195–207). The object is to study, describe, and understand the past, without seeking a philosophic, spiritual, or religious unity in history. History no longer carries a burden from the Enlightenment. It uses a critical, disciplined inquiry to study the past. Its practitioners are legion.

Biblical criticism, influenced by secular historical research, developed and refined its techniques. They are still part of the common coin of all interpretation today. The historical exegesis demanded by Semler, Gabler, and Keil received a decisive impulse forward from Friedrich Schleiermacher. He provided a systematic analysis of the process of understanding in his *Hermeneutik* (published 1838), which gave confidence that historical criticism has a positive effect (Richardson, p. 79). Schleiermacher's great prestige made the use of philological and historical methods respectable in Germany. Biblical studies shifted to the universities, where a new sense of freedom made impartial and objective research the ideal.[49] Interpretation of the Bible was now "uncompromisingly historical, . . . that struggled to determine what the writer intended to say and the first readers could and must have understood. . . ." (Kümmel, *Erbe*, p. 872). This ideal also influenced those who carried on exegesis for theological reasons.

Text criticism made great advances. Karl Lachmann, a classicist influenced by Schleiermacher, produced the first truly

49. Grant, *The Bible in the Church*, p. 131. Bengel, teacher in the Klosterschule at Denkendorf, refused university calls a century earlier.

critical text of the New Testament (1831), and, in the second edition (1842–1850), provided an extensive apparatus with suggestions on method.[50] The editions of the theologians Tischendorff (1872) and Westcott and Hort (1882) served generations of scholarship.[51] Rudolf Kittel produced the first edition of the standard critical text of the Hebrew Old Testament, presently being revised under the editorship of Karl Elliger and Wilhelm Rudolph.[52] Reliable texts, the basis of all historical work, are a major contribution of the nineteenth century.

In 1829 Heinrich August Wilhelm Meyer issued volume one of his *Critical and Exegetical Commentary*, a series still alive after numerous revisions. In the preface he stated that exegesis should be free of dogmatic and party spirit, not captive to any kind of "-ism" (supernaturalism, naturalism, or rationalism). The exegete should determine historically and grammatically what his author said, no more and no less.[53] In England J. B. Lightfoot, B. F. Westcott, and F. J. A. Hort wrote commentaries that were critical, linguistic, historical, and exegetical rather than edifying, yet done by Christians for Christians. Influenced by the scholarly tradition of the classicist Richard Porson these commentaries set a standard in England and Scotland for meticulous attention to detail, careful philological precision, and sober historical discrimination (Neill, pp. 86–89). By the end of the century *The International Critical Commentary* and the *Handkommentar* on Old and New Testaments stood next to the Meyer series.

The works written by David Friedrich Strauss and Ferdinand Christian Baur incited many to historical study. Strauss began the "really significant era of criticism of the New Testa-

---

50. Lachmann also published a landmark edition of Lucretius. See Kümmel, *NT*, pp. 146–148, 481. The production of great critical editions was a hallmark of nineteenth-century scholarship. The *Corpus Reformatorum* (Melanchthon, Calvin, Zwingli), the Erlangen and Weimar editions of Luther, the Berlin and Vienna corpora of the early Fathers, the *Bibliotheca Teubneriana*, the Migne *Patrologiae*, the *Corpus Scriptorum Historiae Byzantinae*, the great inscription collections (CIG, IG, CIL), and many other such collections originated in this century. The work provided new standards for textual editions.

51. Neill, *Interpretation*, pp. 69–76; B. M. Metzger, *The Text of the New Testament* (2d ed. New York: Oxford University Press, 1968), pp. 126–135.

52. *Biblia Hebraica Stuttgartiensia* (Stuttgart: Württembergische Bibelanstalt). The great Cambridge Septuagint, still incomplete, began in this century.

53. Ernst, "Das hermeneutische Problem," p. 32; Kümmel, *Erbe*, p. 371; *NT*, p. 111.

ment" with the publication of *Das Leben Jesu* (1835).[54] Strauss, in part still a child of rationalism, followed Reimarus in denying the historicity of all miracles, the resurrection, and most of the content of the Gospels. However, he tried to save the eternal truths contained in the historically dubious materials through the concept of myth (Ernst, pp. 33–34). Reason destroys truth by its naturalistic explanations; the use of myth allows the preservation of truth in the face of rationalism. Myth allowed Strauss to place the Gospels into their own conceptual world and save their writers from being deceivers. It allowed him to read the Gospels without imposing on them modern presuppositions. *Das Leben Jesu* was a shocking work that roused a storm of protest. The clash between consistent historical study with rationalist presuppositions and the revelation-claim of the Bible was very clear. The conclusions Strauss reached were radical and questionable, but forced the issues of method and source criticism on scholarship and so were a factor in the origins of a truly historical approach.[55]

Ferdinand Christian Baur took up the challenge and produced the first history of early Christianity written on the basis of historical criticism.[56] As a teacher in the Gymnasium at Maulbronn (where he taught Strauss Roman history), Baur learned to appreciate Neibuhr's source criticism. He used this method on the New Testament to put the sources into chronological order, and on that basis to write the history of the early church. He concluded that Paul—whose letters were limited to Romans, Corinthians, and Galatians—is *the* primary source for this history, that the conflicting parties in the early church are reflected in the New Testament itself, and that history is to be understood as a sequence of interrelated causes and effects. History is to be written to understand Christianity as an histor-

---

54. A. R. C. Leaney, *Biblical Criticism*, ed. R. P. C. Hanson (Baltimore: Penguin Books, 1970), p. 233. Strauss was translated into English by George Eliot (1846, reissued by Fortress Press in 1973).

55. Good short critiques of Strauss are found in Kümmel, *NT*, pp. 120–127; Wilckens, *Was heisst Auslegung*, pp. 100–104; Neill, *Interpretation*, pp. 14–18. For more extensive treatment see Ernst Wolf, "Die Verlegenheit der Theologie. David Friedrich Strauss und die Bibelkritik," *Libertas Christiana. Festschrift F. Delekat* (München: Chr. Kaiser Verlag, 1957), pp. 219–239, and H. Harris, *David Friedrich Strauss and His Theology* (Cambridge: at the University Press, 1973).

56. There are excellent discussions in Scholder, *Baur* (above, note 46), pp. 443–458; Heinz Liebing, "Historical-Critical Theology," *Journal for Theology and Church*, 3 (1967): 55–69; Neill, *Interpretation*, pp. 18–28.

ical religion, not to extract eternal ideas from the history. Investigation which was truly historical had arrived.

For Baur the New Testament was not isolated from the thought currents of the early church. He described these currents in Hegelian terms as thesis (Judeo-Christianity, Peter and Matthew), antithesis (Pauline Christianity), and synthesis (early catholicism). His solution still has currency. His *Tendenzkritik* persuaded him that the entire New Testament is interpretation from beginning to end. Baur left behind him a commitment to source criticism (including *Tendenzkritik*), to an objective presentation of what happened, and to the unity of history (Scholder, *Baur*, pp. 443–447; Neill, pp. 25–28). In Wilckens's opinion (p. 104) these factors make him the father of all modern biblical interpretation. After Baur the methods of Niebuhr and von Ranke were accepted as the proper tools for study of the Bible. Eduard Zeller so evaluated his work in retrospect (1865), and his evaluation is correct (cited in Scholder, *Baur*, p. 436).

Baur's view of the nature of historical unity did not survive, nor did many of his solutions. But he set the questions and introduced the method that led to better and more persuasive views. In England, Lightfoot's dating of I Clement and Ignatius early in the second century dealt a death blow to Baur's late chronology. Lightfoot's reconstruction has provided the framework ever since.[57] The establishment of the two-source theory of Synoptic interrelations by a line of scholars running from Lachmann (1835) to Holzmann (1863) established the priority of Mark and the use of a common source by Matthew and Luke. Acceptance of Baur's belief in the primacy of Matthew was gone.[58] Harnack argued that the tradition deserved more respect than Baur gave it, while the influential *Einleitung* of Adolf Jülicher (1894) argued that many of Baur's historical judgments had to be given up (Kümmel, *NT*, pp. 174–184). There was consensus by the end of the century that Baur's methods were basically correct. Even the conservative scholars of the salvation-history school used the historical

---

57. Some of the best pages in Neill's book are an appreciation of this great scholar, *Interpretation*, pp. 33–57.
58. Kümmel, *NT*, pp. 147–148, 151–155; Neill, *Interpretation*, pp. 108–111. Ewald, Vatke, Graf, and Wellhausen (1878) established the four-source theory of Pentateuchal origins in Old Testament research. Neil, "The Criticism and Theological Use of the Bible," III, 284; Hahn, *The Old Testament in Modern Research*, pp. 11–36.

method to determine the facts. They differed only in their attempt to keep revelation, the interpretive word, tied closely to the facts.[59]

The problem of the relation of faith and historical knowledge, raised by the salvation-history school, became acute at the end of the century. The domination of the history-of-religions school raised the problem to the level of a major theological debate.[60] The schools saw a sharp difference between the Old and New Testaments. Old Testament scholars were immersed in the world of Near Eastern religion being uncovered by archaeologists. Although New Testament scholarship recognized the influence of post-Old Testament Judaism (apocalyptic), it stressed the influence of hellenistic popular piety, mystery religions, and above all gnosticism. It sought sources for biblical religion in the surrounding world. Its basic outlook was positivistic. The Bible, firmly anchored in its own world, was interpreted as an amalgam of various borrowed motifs, and became a book strange to modern men (Wilckens, pp. 108–110; Neill, pp. 152–160). The wandering nomad, the cultic prophet, and the apocalyptic Preacher Jesus were far removed from what piety and religious art had pictured for centuries. The objectified Bible became a foreign book.

The implications were drawn in drastic form. Franz Overbeck called for a "purely historical investigation" that had nothing to do with faith (1871), for scientific study of the Bible demands historical criticism, and that makes the Christian use of the Bible impossible, according to Overbeck (Kümmel, NT, pp. 199–201; Wilckens, p. 112). A quarter century later (1897) Wilhelm Wrede concluded that the inevitable result of historical criticism is to remove all distinctive elements from the New Testament, place its study into the history of religions, and make New Testament theology impossible. The gap between university lectern and church pulpit cannot be bridged. Scientific biblical study serves the truth; only as historical truth serves the church does biblical research serve

59. They included J. C. K. von Hofmann, H. Olzhausen, J. T. Beck, H. Cremer, M. Kähler, and A. Schlatter. See Carl Braaten, *History and Hermeneutic* (Philadelphia: Westminster Press, 1966), p. 23; Ernst, "Das hermeneutische Problem," pp. 35–36; Richardson, *The Bible in the Age of Science*, p. 122.
60. See Kümmel, NT, pp. 245–280; Hahn, *The Old Testament in Modern Research*, pp. 83–118. The key scholars were Hermann Gunkel for the Old Testament, R. Reitzenstein, W. Heitmueller, and W. Bousset for the New Testament.

the church.[61] Alfred Loisy raised the same problem for Roman Catholicism. He tried to guarantee the biblical tradition through the church, since historical criticism makes the tradition problematical. His work was condemned by Pius X in *Pascendi dominici gregis* (1907), thus delaying for decades the formal acceptance of historical methods by the Catholic church.

Historical criticism reigned supreme in Protestantism on the continent at the end of the century. It had been radicalized to a strictly historical discipline, free, independent, and in no way responsible to the church. Although there was opposition from such men as Martin Kähler, Adolf Schlatter, and Rudolf Hermann, Troeltsch's view that history had triumphed was correct. There was to be no significant change until after World War I.[62]

In England and America the history of biblical criticism took a different course. There was a growing use of historical method but little excitement until the publication of *Essays and Reviews* (1860). An article by Benjamin Jowett (later distinguished as a translator of Plato) raised the question whether the Bible should be read like any other book or not. In spite of a spate of protests, the patient historical work of Lightfoot, Westcott, Hort, and others like them showed that historical criticism need not be destructive. By the end of the nineteenth century it had become a part of the theological curricula. Scholars such as S. R. Driver, William Sanday, and W. Robertson Smith were making significant contributions to critical scholarship. The heresy trial of Smith in 1881 was an attempt to change the flow of history, but it did not succeed, largely because the British scholars combined pastoral concern with historical criticism. They had so illuminated the Bible for the average reader that he no longer believed that criticism was destructive or harmful.[63]

61. Wrede's lecture "The Task and Methods of 'New Testament Theology'" was recently translated by Robert Morgan, *The Nature of New Testament Theology* (London: SCM Press, 1973), pp. 68–116. See also Kümmel, *NT*, pp. 304–305; Wilckens, *Was heisst Auslegung*, pp. 112–114.

62. Cf. Kümmel, *NT*, pp. 309–324; *Erbe*, p. 372; Ernst Troeltsch, "Zur Frage des religiösen Apriori," *Zur religiösen Lage, Religionsphilosophie und Ethik* (Ges. Schr. III; 2. Aufl. Aalen: Scientia Verlag, 1962=1922), pp. 765–766.

63. The story is well told by W. Neil, "The Criticism and Theological Use of the Bible," pp. 278–282, S. Neill, *Interpretation*, pp. 29–32, and

It is difficult to overestimate the significance the nineteenth century has for biblical interpretation. It made historical criticism *the* approved method of interpretation. The result was a revolution of viewpoint in evaluating the Bible. The Scriptures were, so to speak, secularized. The biblical books became historical documents to be studied and questioned like any other ancient sources. The Bible was no longer the criterion for the writing of history; rather history had become the criterion for understanding the Bible.[64] The variety in the Bible was highlighted; its unity had to be discovered and could no longer be presumed. The history it reported was no longer assumed to be everywhere correct. The Bible stood before criticism as defendant before judge. This criticism was largely positivist in orientation, imminentist in its explanations, and incapable of appreciating the category of revelation.

THE NEW FACTOR—THEOLOGICAL CONFRONTATION BETWEEN WORLD WARS

The First World War called into question the optimism of historicism and evolutionary thought. That made it impossible any longer to contain the Bible within the straightjacket of positivism. Karl Barth used that opening to issue a call for theological interpretation.[65] The Bible as human word is open, of course, to historical criticism. But such criticism is only a preliminary step in the task of interpretation. One must wrestle with the text until it speaks to modern man, until the walls between then and now fall down, and God's Word addresses man, for God used this "fallible and faulty human word" to confront man.[66] Barth's call raised anew the question of the relationship of faith to historical method. A broad discussion

---

E. C. Blackman, *Biblical Interpretation* (Philadelphia: Westminster Press, 1957), pp. 131–133. The history of biblical interpretation in America is still to be written. The trial of C. Augustus Briggs for heresy in 1893 did not stop the spread of critical method. The work of Moses Stuart and Edward Robinson deserves to be better known. Grant, *The Bible in the Church*, pp. 137–138, gives some brief remarks.

64. J. Blank, "Geschichte und Heilsgeschichte," *Verändert Interpretation den Glauben?* (Freiburg: Herder, 1972), p. 10.

65. *The Epistle to the Romans* (1919, 2d ed. 1921), trans. E. C. Hoskyns (London: Oxford University Press, 1932).

66. See Kümmel, *NT*, pp. 363–368 for selections from Barth, and pp. 369 ff. for the discussion it aroused. See also *Das Neue Testament im 20. Jahrhundert* (Stuttgart: Verlag Kath. Bibelwerk, 1970), pp. 66–67; Lehmann, "Der hermeneutische Horizont," pp. 49–50 (extensive bibliography); Neill, *Interpretation*, pp. 201–212.

THE RISE OF HISTORICAL CRITICISM

followed. Hans Windisch and A. Oepke in Germany and E. C. Hoskyns in England (Neill, pp. 212–221) supported the position that the exegete deals with an history that has ultimate significance. Faith and history cannot be separated.

Rudolf Bultmann also recognized the poverty of a historicist approach to the New Testament. He shared with Barth a concern for the Word's claim on man and sought to use historical criticism to serve that claim. His solution was an existential interpretation of the New Testament. In the New Testament God confronts man through his Word and calls him to self-understanding and authentic existence. Faith is the decision made in response to that call. Faith is not dependent on historical knowledge. Criticism can be ruthlessly practiced, because it makes the nature of faith clear. Demythologizing the text is an aid in demonstrating this independence of faith from history (Lehmann, pp. 50–53; Neill, pp. 227–235).

Both men have been criticized for undervaluing history. For Barth history appears to be a kind of dispensable prelude. Bultmann's program tends to undervalue the singularity of past events and so is not truly historical (so Wilckens, pp. 121–122). Lehmann (p. 52) and Voegtle[67] agree in the more telling criticism that Bultmann's existential canon makes the conceptual world of the interpreter the criterion of truth in the Scriptures. History is in danger of being interiorized and psychologized. Such history really does not need the past.

During this period form criticism came into use. Its findings supported the conviction that faith and history cannot be unraveled from one another and so supported the need for raising the question of faith. American scholarship remained in some ways unaffected by this theological discussion. Barth was being discussed in theology, but Bultmann's theological program was not given serious attention. The research being done was more purely historical, concerned with the sociological environment of the Scriptures. The Chicago school produced a generation of scholars who combined a knowledge of the Roman world with New Testament research. H. J. Cadbury, F. C. Grant, S. J. Case, and E. J. Goodspeed insisted that there is

67. Anton Voegtle, "Historisch-objecktivierende und existentiale Interpretation: Zum Problem ihrer Zuordnung in der neutestamentlichen Exegese," *Das Evangelium und die Evangelien* (Düsseldorf: Patmos Verlag, 1971), pp. 9–15. See also Van A. Harvey, *The Historian and the Believer* (New York: Macmillan, 1966), pp. 131–146.

no substitute for a detailed knowledge of antiquity as a protection against the faddism introduced by philosophical currents in theology.[68]

By the end of the Second World War historical criticism was firmly established, not to be dislodged by any attack. But the dangers of historicism to faith were also clear. The central problem of the relation of faith and historical method was posed as strongly as ever.

68. Robert M. Grant, "American New Testament Study, 1926–1956," *Journal of Biblical Literature*, 87 (1968): 42–50; E. C. Colwell, "New Testament Scholarship in Prospect," *Journal of Bible and Religion*, 28 (1960): 199–203.

III

Goals and Techniques

Today historical criticism is taken for granted; we cannot go back to a precritical age. The method used in biblical research is that used by contemporary historians. Scholars frequently restate this commonplace.[1] Yet it is anything but clear just what we mean when we use the phrase *historical method* (or as is more usual in biblical studies, *historical criticism*). The term *criticism* has an essentially negative connotation for many people, while the word *history* is ambiguous, being used for everything that ever happened, for methods, phenomena, books, the process of study, etc. Ulrich Wilckens gives the following formal definition of scientific biblical interpretation:

The only scientifically responsible interpretation of the Bible is that investigation of the biblical texts that, with a methodologically consistent use of historical understanding in the present state of its art, seeks via reconstruction to recognize and describe the meaning these texts have had in the context of the tradition history of early Christianity.[2]

This definition places modern exegetical method within the

1. ". . . the liberty of the scientific and critical approach has established itself almost beyond the possibility of cavil." So Stephen Neill, *The Interpretation of the New Testament 1816–1961* (London: Oxford University Press, 1966), pp. 338. ". . . *das schlichte Faktum, dass die Verbindlichkeit der genannten Methode von keinem Bibelwissenschaftler mehr in Zweifel gezogen wird.*" Günter Bornkamm, "Die ökumenische Bedeutung der historisch-kritischen Bibelwissenschaft," *Geschichte und Glaube* (München: Chr. Kaiser Verlag, 1971), II, 13. "At least in Western Christianity . . . the battle for the acceptance of historical criticism as applied to the Bible has been won." R. P. C. Hanson, *Biblical Criticism* (Baltimore: Penguin Books, 1970), pp. 12–13.
2. Ulrich Wilckens, "Über die Bedeutung historischer Kritik in der modernen Bibelexegese," *Was heisst Auslegung der Heiligen Schrift?* (Regensburg: Friedrich Pustet, 1966), p. 133, my translation.

context of historical method in general. An understanding of historical criticism demands a consideration of what historians do today.

WHAT IS HISTORY?

History as a "rational attempt at analysis," as a systematic knowledge of the past, is still very young.[3] The necessary tools only came into being in the eighteenth century.[4] Modern scientific history is systematic knowledge of the past; its object is man's activities in time, space, and society, expressed in a coherent report (usually written). It deals with real events and real men (not abstractions), and the causes of their activities and their influence.[5] History is not abstract knowledge of men (as is philosophy), but a story that moves (Morison, p. 273), best told by narrative rather than statistical or sociological reporting (Hexter, pp. 27–39). The historian deals only with the part of the past that is accessible to him, "that part which he recognizes as amenable to rational explanation and interpretation, and from it draws conclusions which may serve as a guide to action" (Carr, p. 104). The coherence achieved is not a logical, but a narrative coherence, although logic must be used in the process of investigation and reconstruction. The narrative, based on the critical study of all relevant texts and sources, is to illuminate the past actions of man. Critically written narrative is not a mere retelling of what the sources say, but a narrative based on what the sources say after their adequacy, veracity, and intelligibility are questioned.

3. Marc Bloch, *The Historian's Craft*, trans. Peter Putnam (Manchester: Manchester University Press, 1967), p. 13. Jack Hexter makes the same point in "The Rhetoric of History," *Doing History* (Bloomington & London: Indiana University Press, 1971), p. 16. The other professional historians cited in this chapter include E. H. Carr, *What Is History?* (Harmondsworth, Eng.: Penguin Books, 1973=1964); William H. Lucey, *History: Methods and Interpretations* (Chicago: Loyola University Press, 1958); Samuel Eliot Morison, "Faith of a Historian," *The American Historical Review*, 56 (1951): 261–275, cited according to this printing, though reprinted in *By Land and Sea* (New York: Alfred Knopf, 1953), pp. 346–359. The philosophers of history (Collingwood, Croce, etc.) will not be discussed. Van A. Harvey's *The Historian and the Believer* (New York: Macmillan, 1966) is a useful book, especially the first three chapters (pp. 3–101).
4. These include Descartes's principle of doubt and the ancillary disciplines historical geography, genealogy, paleography, sphragistics, numismatics, epigraphy, etc. Cf. A. von Brandt, *Werkzeug des Historikers* (6. Aufl. Stuttgart: W. Kohlhammer, 1971), p. 12.
5. Bloch, *The Historian's Craft*, pp. 23–27; Lucey, *History*, pp. 1–3, 10–12.

The historical-critical method of contemporary biblical scholarship is also young. It arose out of the great reorientation of the human mind that came from the scientific revolution of the fifteenth and sixteenth centuries and the development of historical method in the nineteenth.[6] It produces history in the modern sense, for it consciously and critically investigates biblical documents to write a narrative of the history they reveal. Grant defines its goal as "a narrative which reflects events in a sequence roughly chronological."[7] Biblical scholarship is *critical* because it uses the powers of the mind on the sources with which it deals. This criticism is essentially positive, since it appreciates what it finds. It is "a founded, comparing, contrasting, analyzing response, in other words, discriminating appreciation."[8] It is also a *systematic method*, since it has a clear historical goal in mind and follows a procedure using criteria and presuppositions to reach that goal. There is only one point at which biblical scholarship might conflict with secular historians. The goal of secular history is anthropocentric: the activities of man. In reconstructing the narrative of biblical history, biblical scholarship must ask whether the object includes God's actions with and for man in space and time. Is the biblical view of God *eo ipso* ruled out by the definition of history?

THE GOALS OF THE HISTORIAN

The first goal of all history is to present a "corpus of ascertained fact" that answers the questions "What actually happened, and why?" (Morison, p. 263). Modern history is dominated by a will to truth, and so by the necessity of investigating sources critically to obtain the inferences and judgments that lie behind them (Harvey, pp. 39–42).

However, the historian is concerned with more than the corpus of facts. He wants to illuminate the past, to understand

6. See chapter two. The formulation comes from Alan Richardson, "The Rise of Modern Biblical Scholarship and Recent Discussions of the Authority of the Bible," *The Cambridge History of the Bible*, vol. III: *The West from the Reformation to the Present Day* (Cambridge: at the University Press, 1963), p. 295; *The Bible in the Age of Science* (London: SCM Press, 1961), pp. 9–76.
7. Robert Grant, *A Historical Introduction to the New Testament* (London: Collins, 1963), p. 74.
8. K. Grobel, "Biblical Criticism," *The Interpreter's Dictionary of the Bible* (New York/Nashville: Abingdon Press, 1962), I, 407. Cf. G. Eldon Ladd, *The New Testament and Criticism* (Grand Rapids: Wm. B. Eerdmans, 1967), p. 13: ". . . making intelligent judgments . . . in the light of all the available evidence. . . ."

the events, and to interpret them.[9] He aims to create as comprehensive a picture as possible of a culture's account of its past.[10] To do that he must help his readers to follow the movement and tempo of events, grasp the motives as well as the actions of men, identify the imperatives that move men to action (as distinguished from the pseudo-imperatives), recognize the role of accident, catastrophe, or luck, and know what the participants conceived the stakes to be. To achieve that, argues Hexter, the historian must use language that is not denotative, as scientific language is, but connotative, evocative, and less than scientifically accurate.[11] Such language is more appropriate to a clear, understandable presentation of history than is the bloodless language of science. Narrative may sacrifice some historical detail, yet is usually the best way to achieve the desired goals.

The goal of history is explanation and understanding, not the passing of judgment on the moral acts of individuals. Understanding is not ethics; that is a task of philosophy and theology. The historian can evaluate events, institutions, or policies in terms of their effectiveness. He can strike a balance between gain and loss. But he recognizes that the task of history is not judgment, but description and explanation. He must understand and point out the mistakes of those whom he loves, and recognize the motives and accomplishments of those he dislikes. (Carr, pp. 75–81; Bloch, pp. 138–142; Morison, p. 269.)

Understanding is not etiology. It is valuable to know the source of an idea or movement; but it can lead to confusing "ancestry with explanation" (Bloch, p. 32). In explanation the horizontal dimension is as significant as the vertical. The historian must explan why an idea borrowed from some earlier source becomes significant at a particular time and place in history, no sooner and no later.

History has a restricted goal. The historian cannot know all

9. Droysen was a lifelong critic of von Ranke and his school because he felt von Ranke reduced history to the mere accumulation of facts. See the letters of 1837 to 1857 cited in J. G. Droysen, *Texte zur Geschichtstheorie*, ed. Günter Birtsch and Jörn Rüsen (Göttingen: Vandenhoeck & Ruprecht, 1972), pp. 81–83.

10. J. Huizinga, as cited by von Brandt, *Werkzeug*, p. 9.

11. Hexter, *Doing History*, pp. 25–27; Bloch, *The Historian's Craft*, p. 104, speaks of "the idol of false precision."

there is to know, since he is handicapped by his sources and his own manner of viewing them. In a sense the historian creates his facts, calling them back from the sources. But significant facts may not be recoverable from the sources, e.g., the physical characteristics of Jesus or the names of his teachers. Some "facts" will not fit into the historian's rational pattern of explanation. Thus the historian produces only a "reduced representation of the past" (the phrase is Morison's, p. 265). His sources and mode of explanation lead to a selection of what can be known. He selects only what leads to the generalizations and conclusions of his purpose in writing. This reduction by selection is influenced by the questions he and his contemporaries are asking. His view is a limited but true one—much as an artist's landscape is true although it does not represent all the eye can see.[12]

The goals of the biblical student are those of historians in general, a corpus of facts arranged in narrative to give an explanation of the past. He tries to answer the questions "What actually happened?" and "Why?" about events reported in the Bible.[13] Biblical history has a double aspect. The books themselves have a history that must be set into the framework of Israelite and nascent Christian history. The Bible also narrates a history, which, of course, lies at an earlier stage than the books themselves. Both aspects must be investigated and used in the writing of the narrative account of Israel, Jesus, or the primitive church.[14]

To gather the corpus of facts which he needs and to write the narrative the scholar must have a firm chronological structure; chronology is the skeleton of history. History cannot be

12. Carr, *What Is History?* pp. 10–30, on historical facts. His words on selection, p. 105:
History therefore is a process of selection in terms of historical significance. . . . history is "a selective system" not only of cognitive, but of causal, orientations to reality. . . . the standard of historical significance is his ability to fit them into his pattern of rational explanation and interpretation. Other sequences of cause and effect have to be rejected as accidental, not because the relation of cause and effect is different, but because the sequence itself is irrelevant.

13. These are not his only goals! He also has the goal of the literary commentator, to state what the texts he uses say, and that of the theologian, to make clear the proclamation that is contained in them.

14. E. Krentz, "Hermeneutics and the Teacher of Theology," *Concordia Theological Monthly*, 42 (1971): 269–271.

written without it, for chronological factors determine whether a theory of causation is possible and the direction in which, other factors being equal, dependence must flow.[15]

Students are often surprised to discover that chronological reconstruction in many cases hangs by a slender thread. New Testament history is to a large degree written in relation to Acts and the Pauline corpus. Other documents are related to that history. The one fixed point in Paul's life is derived from the Gallio inscription found at Delphi in 1897 (the five fragments first being published in 1905). The inscription is dated in the twenty-sixth acclamation of the Emperor Claudius; the acclamation is not referred to in ancient literary sources but its approximate date can be determined from the datable acclamations before and after it. The normal term of office for a proconsul in a senatorial province was one year, from spring to spring. The probable date of Lucius Junius Gallio's term as proconsul is spring, 51 to spring, 52. By correlating the data of Acts 18:11 with Gallio's term the probable dates for the ministry of Paul in Corinth can be inferred. All other dates in Paul's life are fixed by working backward and forward from the Corinthian ministry. The date depends on a number of assumptions: that Acts is accurate; that no unusual or chance factors gave Gallio a longer term or a second term; that the number of acclamations celebrated by Claudius in one year did not exceed three, etc. New Testament chronology depends on the fortuitous survival of five small fragments of a stone inscription.[16]

The corpus of facts includes the historical setting in which the documents were written and the events took place. The Old Testament reflects in its various parts semi-nomadic life, Near Eastern village culture, and the urban society of the time. The New Testament came into existence in a world

15. Grant, *Historical Introduction,* p. 74. O. Cullmann, "The Necessity and Function of Higher Criticism," *The Early Church,* ed. A. J. B. Higgins (Philadelphia: Westminster Press, 1956), pp. 11–12. Cullmann adds that chronology will "bring out the historical sequence into the light of day, so that the divine plan (what the New Testament calls *oikonomia*) may become evident not *behind* but *within* history itself." This theological aim is a statement of faith, not of historical criticism.

16. For orientation in chronology see Beda Rigaux, *Letters of St. Paul,* trans. S. Yonick (Chicago: Franciscan Herald Press, 1968), chap. IV, pp. 68–71. G. B. Caird, "Chronology of the New Testament, *The Interpreter's Dictionary of the Bible* (New York/Nashville: Abingdon Press, 1962), I, 599–607; S. J. De Vries, "Chronology of the Old Testament," ibid., 580–599.

where cultural influences from East and West were mingling, fertilizing, interacting, and conflicting with one another. Its narrative begins in Palestinian Judaism, moves to urban Greece and Asia Minor, and concludes in the broad reaches of the Roman Empire. Setting the narrative within its social and cultural context prevents history from turning into the study of abstract ideas. It places biblical history into the stream of the general story of man, and thus shows what is unique in it and what unites it with the history and culture around it. It helps to clarify the movement of thought and, incidentally, to remove many difficulties in the language and thought of the Bible.[17]

The writing of biblical history demonstrates the Bible's complexity. It should also explain how the diversity of thought, formulation, and action arose out of the life of Israel and the church in their political, social, and religious milieus. The interpreter indicates the possible cultural borrowings from the surrounding peoples without holding that genetic relationships necessarily constitute explanations. He seeks not only what is unique in biblical history, although the unique is particularly interesting and valuable, but also the explanation, the reconstruction of the occurrences in such a way as to understand the rise and development of the distinctive mixture of autochthonous and imported elements that are found in Israel and the church at any particular time or place.

The first task of the historian who wishes to meet this goal is simply to hear the texts with which he is working. He uses every linguistic tool at his disposal to determine the sense the text had for its writer and first audience (the *sensus literalis sive historicus*). He seeks to hear the text apart from the mass of biblical interpretation that has been laid over it in the history of its use. This basic respect for the historical integrity of a text is inherent in all historical criticism.[18]

17. Grant, *Historical Introduction*, pp. 84–86; Kurt Frör, *Biblische Hermeneutik* (München: Chr. Kaiser Verlag, 1961), p. 49; A. R. C. Leaney, *Biblical Criticism* (above, note 1), p. 169; Cullmann, "Higher Criticism," p. 13.
18. Richardson, "Rise of . . . Scholarship," p. 304. James Smart, *The Strange Silence of the Bible in the Church* (Philadelphia: Westminster Press, 1970), p. 59. This determination to hear a text out on its own terms may mean that an interpretation long held has to be given up. This fact has at times given historical criticism a bad name in the church; criticism appears to be destructive—although in reality it is, in the literal sense, a most conservative process, since historical research conserves the textual data.

An example may illustrate the point. Paul almost casually mentions a "collection for the saints" in 1 Cor. 16:1–4 and gives brief directions for its gathering. In 2 Corinthians 8 and 9 he urges the quick completion of the "ministry to the saints" under the leadership of Titus, while Rom. 15:25–29 describes his plan to go to Jerusalem with the "contribution for the poor among the saints in Jerusalem" (RSV). The immediate modern tendency is to identify this collection with some kind of inner Christian relief program for the destitute.

But first-century Christians might have heard something quite different.[19] The agreement between Paul, Peter, and James at the Jerusalem Council included the provision that Paul should remember "the poor" (*hoi ptôchoi*, Gal. 2:10). Paul himself says he was eager to do so. These poor may not have been the economically deprived, but the Jewish-Christian community in Jerusalem. The term *ptôchos* is used of the disciples in the beatitudes (Matt. 5:3=Lk. 6:20). Later the term is used to designate a particular branch of Jewish Christians (Ebionites). The collection was to support the original Jerusalem congregation, as Rom. 15:26 suggests. (It should be translated "the poor who are the saints in Jerusalem.") "The poor" then are synonymous with the "saints" in 1 Cor. 16:1.[20]

The collection has much greater significance than the expression of caritative concern. Jewish eschatology anticipated that the wealth of the nations would flow to Jerusalem (Is. 60:5, 61:6, 66:12; Ps. 72:10–15, *Or. Sib.* III.772–773). Paul's companions in Acts 20:4 all have Gentile names. It is a Gentile collection (1 Cor. 16:1; 2 Cor. 8:1, 9:2), as the stress on the names Galatia, Macedonia, and Achaia suggests. Even *poor* Gentiles are contributing (2 Cor. 8:14). The collection then shows that Paul's proclamation is bringing eschatological hopes to fulfillment—and Paul's ministry to the Gentiles (Gal. 2:10) is vindicated.

The example illustrates that the historical context often demands an interpretation that is not expected from the van-

19. On this issue see Keith Nickle, *The Collection. A Study in Paul's Strategy* (London: SCM Press, 1966); Dieter Georgi, *Die Geschichte der Kollekte des Paulus für Jerusalem* (Hamburg: Herbert Reich, 1964).

20. Support for this interpretation might be found in C. K. Barrett's suggestion that the terminology in Gal. 2:1–10 reflects the view that the Jerusalem church is the eschatological temple. "The poor" is also an eschatological term. "Paul and the Pillar Apostles," *Studia Paulina in honorem Johannis de Zwaan* (Haarlem: de Erven F. Bohn, 1953), pp. 1–19.

tage point of the interpreter's own time and culture. We can thus expand our description to say that hearing texts on their own terms is not only the first, but even the "fundamental act of all textual interpretation."[21] It is the essential basis for all other use of the text, both in historical scholarship and in the proclamatory mission of the church.

Are there no specifically Christian goals for the critical interpretation of the Bible? Wilckens describes the goal of the historical method as "the recognition of early Christian history as the history of the origin of Christianity, to which we belong today" (p. 133). Wilckens has been criticized for setting a goal that may prejudice the task of gathering facts. But it is a desirable goal! A corpus of facts and an adequate narrative explanation for them are prerequisite historical goals. But the historian also works (in part) to arrive at an understanding of himself and man through an understanding of the past. That self-understanding which arises out of the Bible, the basic documents of the Christian faith, would indeed include the goal that Wilckens sets. It can still be objective history.

THE HISTORIAN'S METHODS: TOOLS AND TECHNIQUES

Historical criticism serves the historian's need for valid, reliable evidence by enabling him to establish whether or not testimony actually was given by a competent and reliable witness. It is a method for *collecting* all possible witnesses to an era or event, *evaluating* what they say, *relating* the findings to one another in a coherent structure, and *presenting* the conclusion with the evidence (Lucey, pp. 19 and 22). Historical criticism is more than the application of common sense to the past, since common sense is generally the reflection of the momentary perspective at a level of external observation. It is not yet criticism, observes Bloch (p. 80), merely to refuse to take all documents at face value.

Collecting materials is both a heuristic and a taxonomical procedure. In his search for all relevant sources the historian must know the types that may be useful and form an attitude toward them. He distinguishes between remains (tangible remnants of man's social and economic life, of things made for

21. Anton Voegtle, "Historisch-objektivierende und existentiale Interpretation: Zum Problem ihrer Zuordnung in der neutestamentlichen Exegese," *Das Evangelium und die Evangelien* (Düsseldorf: Patmos Verlag, 1971), p. 12.

immediate use, not posterity) and records (materials consciously produced to inform or mold contemporary or subsequent opinion). He values remains for their objectivity (Lucey, pp. 27–32; Grant, p. 76).

Sources are not themselves history and do not give immediate access to history.[22] The source survives and is examined in our twentieth-century world; it is no longer in its original context. It is a historicist delusion to think that we can ever actually see it, read it, or use it in the original frame of reference. Even the artifact found by the archaeologist in its stratum is no longer seen in the context of use in the living society for which it was made. Palestinian archaeologists find small round potters' disks in large numbers; they call them either gaming pieces or bottle stoppers. The truth is, no one knows what this artifact (found in the thousands) tells us, since the context of use is lost.

Moreover, what remains is always only a thirsty fragment of the past. All our sources are like the buildings excavated by archaeologists, whose size, decoration, and function have to be reconstructed from the bits and fragments that survive. The farther back the historian's interest goes, the more deficient his sources are.

Historical sources are like witnesses in a court of law: they must be interrogated and their answers evaluated. The art of interrogation and evaluation is called criticism.[23] In external criticism the historian examines the credentials of a witness to determine the person's credibility (authenticity) and whether the evidence has come down unimpaired (integrity). Dates given must be verified; if absent they must be supplied (as far

22. Harvey, *The Historian and the Believer*, p. 69. R. Lapointe, *Les trois dimensions de l'hermeneutique* (Paris: J. Gabalda, 1967) quotes a striking illustration from H. Marrou: "The graffiti found on the wall of a Herculaneum villa (*Apollonius, medicus, titi imp[eratoris], hic cacavit bene*) is not the event itself, but only a partial survival of the event."
23. The term has a long history. In antiquity it denoted the expert's exercise of his logical faculties on his special area of knowledge or thought (cf. Sextus Empiricus, *Adv. Math.* I.79 and 248). The negative connotation in contemporary usage is the result of eighteenth-century dualism— the separation of the true from the false, the genuine from the spurious, the beautiful from the ugly, or the lawful from the unlawful. At first it was possible to unite the critic and the Christian in one person, but the negative connotation the term *criticism* suffered under since the eighteenth century seemed to make criticism and Christianity incompatible. See the excellent compressed history in Reinhart Kosselleck, *Kritik und Krise. Eine Studie zur Pathogenese der bürgerlichen Welt* (Suhrkamp Taschenbuch, 1973), pp. 85–103.

as possible) from internal references to persons, institutions or events, from stylistics, or from quotations made. The historian seeks information as complete as possible not in order to discredit his source, but to understand its credibility and use its witness. There are no rules of thumb for determining authenticity; the skilled judgment of the knowledgeable historian must serve as guide. The content, history of transmission, script, or appearance (in an autograph), and other factors may aid. An anonymous document is not less valuable than one whose author is known; the *Hellenica Oxyrhynchia* is an outstanding source for Greek history, although its author is unknown (Theopompus?).

The historian does not lose interest in a document that is not authentic. It is also an historical source and gives knowledge about its unknown author and his interests (or those of the group he represents). The historian seeks to determine and understand the motivation behind the forgery; in that way, inadvertently and against the author's will a spurious document reveals aspects of its actual time and place of origin. Such unintentional information is very valuable.[24]

An authentic document may suffer corruption in the process of transmission. A part of a document may be unintentionally destroyed (the conclusion of Mark?) or a copyist may simply misread his text. However, a block of material may be inserted intentionally into an otherwise authentic document in order to clothe it with the authentic author's authority. Authentic fragments from different works may be combined in order to preserve them (2 Corinthians?). In all these cases the tests of literary criticism and historical reliability must be applied. Where corruption is established, the scholar seeks to determine the cause or purpose of intentional contamination.

External criticism of origin and integrity is a preliminary to internal criticism, the determination of the original sense and the evaluation of the competence and honesty of the witness. The first task is to hear the witness or author as precisely as possible. The historian's criticism begins with the text itself, not however to measure the emotional or rhetorical effect of the work, but to understand its content as a testimony to past

24. On authenticity and forgery see Bloch, *The Historian's Craft*, pp 90–99, Lucey, *History*, pp. 46–69; Grant, *Historical Introduction*, pp. 77–78. One must not import false standards of authorship into a different age or culture.

human experience and action.[25] The historian uses all the linguistic tools available to determine the meaning the text had for its first hearers at the time of original composition (intended sense). Knowledge of the author's education, character, age, background, personal experiences, emotional state and ambitions, the circumstances that led to the writing, and the occasion for which it was to be used all help to illuminate the intended sense (Lucey, pp. 71–73).

Evaluation of what is said follows. The writer's position as an observer, his internal consistency, his bias or prejudices, and his abilities as a writer all affect the accuracy of what he knows and the competence of the report. Where more than one report exists, they must be compared. If they disagree, this does not automatically mean that one is wrong. Differences may arise from the writers' position for observation. If two sources agree too closely, one is suspect as being an uncredited copy of another (Bloch, pp. 99–104). The historian looks for substantial truth; errors in detail do not discredit a witness.

The historian puts great trust in involuntary witnesses that were not intended to transmit information. The economic history of Roman Egypt is better recovered from the business documents included in papyrus finds than from the remarks of ancient historians. Inflation is witnessed in the debasing of metal in coinage. The great fresco in the Villa of the Mysteries at Pompei is a most significant document for the history of Roman religion in the first century. It was not designed for curious outsiders' eyes. The evidence of the synagogue mosaics discovered in the last century must be used when the religion of Palestinian Judaism from A.D. 70 to 500 is discussed. The use of the God Helios and the signs of the Zodiac, the iconography of the binding of Isaac at Beit Alpha, and the inscriptions recording the names and titles of donors are valuable because they were not designed to describe Judaism to a later, Gentile audience. Involuntary witnesses give us access to an otherwise lost past.

Despite our inevitable subordination to the past, we have freed ourselves at least to the extent that, eternally condemned to know

25. The goals of literary criticism are well described in René Wellek and Austin Warren, *Theory of Literature* (Harmondsworth: Penguin Books, 1973), p. 139. Concern for literary figures, genres, imagery, etc. are used by the historian to judge the historical usefulness of material, not to achieve a literary appreciation of it *per se*.

only by means of its "tracks," we are nevertheless successful in knowing far more of the past than the past itself had thought good to tell us. Properly speaking, it is a glorious victory of mind over its matter. (Bloch, pp. 63–64)

One normally assumes that an author, within the limitations of the culture and morality of his own age, does not willfully lie. But an author who is a poor observer, who has a bad memory, who writes long after the event, or who has reason to conceal material that may harm him, a friend, or his own social group may well bend the truth. Therefore, the historian challenges all sources in a more or less friendly manner, even those he most highly respects! Historical method is a process for determining what really happened and what the significance of past happenings was (and is). When the historian presents his reconstruction of the past, he is obliged to support it with cogent reasoning and persuasive data. Therefore, the historian must not only determine what his witnesses say, but also evaluate their truthfulness. In the process, as E. H. Carr notes (pp. 10–30), the historian decides what the few significant data are, calls them to the level of historical fact by his interpretation of them, and so is engaged in a "continuous process of moulding his facts to his interpretation and his interpretation to his facts" (p. 29). Van Harvey is equally striking in formulation: "The historian *confers* authority upon a witness" (p. 42).

Criticism is often viewed negatively by the nonhistorian. To him the historian appears either to be a suspicious, unfriendly, irascible person or an iconoclast interested only in overturning what people have always known and believed, always revising and changing the past. There is some truth in the fear. "Historical criticism is a form of criticism of the present, a setting into question of the prevailing *sensus communis*."[26] But the impression is basically mistaken. The historian does not change opinion for the sake of change, but for the sake of understanding. Criticism interrogates documents to determine their precise significance. The judgment that a witness is not correct serves the historian's quest for understanding and truth because it is the starting point for the discovery of truth. Every document is relevant to some situation and contains truth

26. Walter Kasper, *Die Methoden der Dogmatik* (München, 1967), p. 52 as cited by Josef Blank, *Verändert Interpretation den Glauben?* (Freiburg: Herder, 1972), p. 32.

about it. The historian's task is to learn that truth (Bloch, pp. 89–90).

In historical research understanding the past means putting it into a significant structure that can be communicated to others. The historian seeks all possible explanations for the facts he regards as significant, looks at the facts in the light of these explanations, and then eliminates all explanations that do not adequately account for the data. In presenting his explanation he also presents the supporting data.

Two significant recent contributions from different perspectives show the nature of this supporting data. Van Harvey points out that the historian uses various forms of argumentation because his subject matter covers different fields (each field has a type of justification or warrant peculiar to it). History is adequately presented when the arguments achieve "whatever cogency or well-foundedness can relevantly be asked for in that field."[27] It cannot be measured by the criteria of any one scientific or philosophic position. Historical argument is much like legal argument; it depends on the soundness of judgment of the historian, who asks what explanation derives from the data, corresponds to generally accepted warrants or backup statements, and what kind of assent it compels (pp. 59–64). Historical argumentation deals not with the logically possible, but with what is likely under the given conditions.

J. H. Hexter points out in a significant essay that historians have paid almost no attention to the proper language or method of presenting history.[28] He argues for a model of presentation that is indebted more to the connotative language of rhetoric than to the denotative language of science and philosophy. Narrative is closer to rhetoric because it awakens reactions that are an aid to historical explanation (pp. 29–30). Narrative provides adequate historical tempo with the proper expansions or contractions of scale appropriate to history as seen in retrospect (p. 38).

Both Harvey and Hexter see that the sound judgment of the historian is needed for proper historical explanation. What are the qualifications of the good historian? He is curious, full of questions about the past. He possesses the necessary intellectual knowledge to use historical sources with proper method.

27. Harvey, *The Historian and the Believer*, p. 48.
28. "The Rhetoric of History," *Doing History* (Bloomington & London: Indiana University Press, 1971), pp. 15–76.

He can think critically, interrogating and evaluating the sources so as to answer the questions he has posed and to discover newer, better questions to ask (von Brandt, p. 9). These qualities do not make an historian, but one cannot be an historian without them.

The historian must be a man of absolute honesty with a passion for the truth, for "truth about the past is the essence of history" (Morison, p. 262). This concern runs through all historical writing, from Thucydides' determination to present the true causes rather than the pretexts alleged for the Peloponnesian War (I.23.4), through Cicero's statement that the "first law of history is neither to dare to say anything false nor to falsify anything true" (Lucey, p. 15), down to our own time. The passion for truth results in a respect for the records, the documents. An historian is judged by whether his work communicates knowledge. If it does, his work is authentic, true, and validly written (Hexter, pp. 47–48). The historian's commitment to truth and the records forces him to admit that he can only know what is in the records. This respect for the texts creates the climate making possible the discovery of something surprising in the texts to renew, change, and correct the received picture of the past and preventing history from falling into a stereotype (Bloch, p. 86).

The historian has balance and humility. He knows and states, without apology, that his work does not have the objectivity of the natural sciences. He is as skeptical and critical of himself as he is of his sources, for he knows the gaps in the documents and his own tendency to ignore the data that do not fit his own reconstruction. Again Hexter has put it well:

. . . no historian does, and no sensible historian claims to, communicate the whole truth about a man, since there are many things about any man living or dead which no human being, not even the man himself, knows. The full knowledge on which alone a final judgment is possible exists only in the mind of God. (pp. 53–54)

History retains its mystery, its partly inexplicable character, even in the face of the most rigidly critical examination. It also retains its fascination and its ability to surprise. A discipline that is by definition incapable of fully grasping its object, man, leaves its practitioners properly humble and open to new discoveries, new criteria, and even new directions. They need only correspond to the demand for honesty and truth.

47

The differences between biblical scholarship and secular history derive from the major source, the Bible, and not the methods used. Biblical scholars use the methods of secular history on the Bible to discover truth and explain what happened. The methods are secular. The procedures may be modified to fit the Bible, but are not essentially changed.[29]

For example, an appeal to the canon, a carefully circumscribed body of literature, does not settle the question of sources for biblical history. The boundaries of the canon are not the boundaries of the source material for Israelite or primitive Christian history. Restrict yourself to the canon and you will not understand the canon. Extra-biblical literature is the basis of chronology, archaeology illuminates the daily life and cultic fixtures of ancient Israel, and inscriptions and Near Eastern annals give the course of world history in which Israelite history must be fitted. The theology and history of post-exilic Judaism cannot be written without the constant use of Josephus, Philo, Qumran, Apocrypha, pseudepigrapha, Mishnah and Talmud. Jewish Christianity is described in large part from the preaching of Peter and the Clementine literature. It is a debated point whether a knowledge of early gnosticism is necessary to understand Pauline theology.[30] In short, the question of sources is as open in biblical history as in history in general. The canon represents a theological decision, not a decision concerning historical methods or sources.

There are many different types of criticism in use by biblical scholarship. It is not our purpose to provide a *vademecum* of method here. That has been well done many times.[31] Rather

29. Erich Dinkler, "Das Wort Gottes, die Bibel und die wissenschaftliche Methode," *Fragen der wissenschaftlichen Erforschung der Heiligen Schrift*, Sonderdruck aus dem Protokoll der Landessynode der Evangelischen Kirche im Rheinland (January, 1962), p. 6.
30. Stephen Neill, *Interpretation*, pp. 157–181. The problem of sources has been illuminated in James M. Robinson and Helmut Koester, *Trajectories through Early Christianity* (Philadelphia: Fortress Press, 1971). The danger of a phenomenological approach is not entirely avoided in this valuable book.
31. There is basic agreement among the following: William Doty, *Contemporary New Testament Interpretation* (Englewood Cliffs, N.J.: Prentice-Hall, 1972), pp. 79–85; Kurt Frör, *Biblische Hermeneutik* (München: Chr. Kaiser Verlag, 1961, with later reprints); Eduard Haller, "On the Interpretative Task," *Interpretation*, 21 (1967): 158–166; Grobel, "Biblical Criticism," pp. 412–413; Otto Kaiser and W. G. Kümmel, *Exegetical Method*, trans. E. V. N. Goetchius (New York: Seabury Press, 1967); John Reumann, "Methods in Studying the Biblical

we shall briefly state how each criticism relates to the purpose of biblical interpretation and point to additional bibliographic resources.

Textual criticism is necessary to establish an accurate text. A basic requirement for determining an author's intended sense is the possession of the text in the form it had when it left its author's hand. Textual criticism also aids in the discovery and removal of unintentional corruptions arising in scribal transmission and intentional corruptions through interpolation. The most famous case in the New Testament is the original ending of Romans. The problem is caused by the wandering doxology (possibly not authentic).[32]

Philological study is of basic importance for determining the intended sense. Historical grammar and lexicography are important for understanding a text like the Bible that is written in ancient languages.[33] Philology includes far more than the study of vocabulary, morphology, and syntax. It has a long and honored history as the general term to describe the study of the forms, significance, and meaning of language and literature.

Literary criticism is used in different senses. In its classical sense it denotes the study and evaluation of literature as artistic production. It treats the rhetorical, poetic, and compositional devices used by an author to structure his thought and

Text Today," *Concordia Theological Monthly*, 40 (1969): 663–670, with an interesting chart to describe the process; Erich Zenger, "Ein Beispiel exegetischer Methoden aus dem Alten Testament," pp. 97–148; Adolf Smitmans, "Ein Beispiel exegetischer Methoden aus dem Neuen Testament," pp. 149–193, both in Josef Schreiner, ed., *Einführung in die Methoden der biblischen Exegese* (Tyrolia: Echter Verlag, 1971); Peter Stuhlmacher, "Zur Methoden- und Sachproblematik einer konfessionellen Auslegung des Neuen Testaments," *Evangelisch-Katholischer Kommentar zum Neuen Testament. Vorarbeiten*, Heft 4 (Zürich, Einsiedeln, Köln: Benziger Verlag; Neukirchen: Neukirchener Verlag, 1972), pp. 22–45, with stress on the problems in each technique; Heinrich Zimmermann, *Neutestamentliche Methodenlehre. Darstellung der historisch-kritischen Methode* (4. Aufl., Stuttgart: Verlag Kath. Bibelwerk, 1974).

32. Ralph Klein, *Textual Criticism of the Old Testament* (Philadelphia: Fortress Press, 1974); Bruce M. Metzger, *The Text of the New Testament* (2d ed. New York: Oxford University Press, 1968); Stuhlmacher, "Zur Methoden," pp. 27–29.

33. Unfortunately many students never get past the linguistic study and competence of the first, basic course in Hebrew or in Greek. Such courses are based on synchronic grammar out of pedagogical necessity. Diachronic grammar and lexicography clarify the growth and development of a language. While it is possible to overstress the koine nature of New Testament Greek (see Stuhlmacher's strictures on Bauer's *Lexicon*, in his "Zur Methoden," pp. 24–25), it is Greek and part of the history of that language.

embellish it with suitable language. Ancient literary critics concentrated their interest on this aspect of literature.[34] It ought to be called back into relevance among modern exegetical techniques. Ancient interests are not always outmoded.[35]

Usually literary criticism is defined more narrowly as the study of sources (more properly called source criticism). Heinrich Zimmermann (p. 85) has called for limiting the term to this sense (for the sake of clarity) and Stuhlmacher supports him (p. 30).[36] The tools source criticism uses are the identification of linguistic and stylistic peculiarities, theological or conceptual variations, logical hiatus or digression, etc. (Grobel, p. 412). The four-source theory of Pentateuchal origins and the two-source theory of Synoptic interrelationships are its major results.[37] Literary (source) criticism has achieved a more sharply contoured profile of the various sources and books, and the authors who stand behind them. It is indispensable for any responsible interpretation of the Bible.[38]

Form criticism identifies and classifies units of (oral) material and relates them to their presumed sociological setting in the earlier life of the community.[39] It seeks to determine how

34. B. F. C. Atkinson, *Literary Criticism in Antiquity* (Cambridge: at the University Press, 1934; reprint London: Methuen, 1952).

35. A knowledge of the "figures of speech" and the "figures of thought" would enrich many commentaries. John Reumann, "Methods," p. 665, calls for a renewal of this study. He ought to be heeded. Cf. Doty, *Contemporary New Testament Interpretation*, p. 77. Neglect of this side of literary criticism derives from the lack of the discipline of classical philology among most biblical scholars. See also William A. Beardslee, *Literary Criticism of the New Testament* (Philadelphia: Fortress Press, 1970).

36. Doty, *Contemporary New Testament Interpretation* (p. 57), notes that this German usage has come to dominate in America. He remarks (p. 53) that one result of source criticism in the eighteenth century was "that the main insights of literary analysis—observations about the function of the literary form or its place of origin in the community—were often lost."

37. Herbert F. Hahn, *The Old Testament in Modern Research*, with a survey of recent literature by Horace D. Hummel (Philadelphia: Fortress Press, 1966), pp. 11–43; W. G. Kümmel, *The New Testament: The History of the Investigation of Its Problems*, trans. S. McLean Gilmour and Howard C. Kee (Nashville/New York: Abingdon Press, 1972), pp. 147–155; Neill, *Interpretation*, pp. 108–127; and the standard Old and New Testament introductions.

38. Norman C. Habel, *Literary Criticism of the Old Testament* (Philadelphia: Fortress Press, 1971); Beardslee, *Literary Criticism of the New Testament*.

39. This is not the same as sociological interpretation, although it has points of contact. See Hahn, *The Old Testament in Modern Research*, pp. 157–184; Dietrich Gewalt, "Neutestamentliche Exegese und Soziologie," *Evangelische Theologie*, 31 (1971): 87–99. On form criticism see Gene

the use in this sociological setting has modified or shaped the tradition.

Redaction criticism studies the contribution of the final writer who composed a literary work on the basis of the sources (oral or written).[40] It is in essence a form of *Tendenzkritik* that uses the editorial techniques of the final writer to determine the special interests and concerns that motivated his work. It compares the form of the final work with its sources to identify the editor's or author's hand. Structural analysis of the document is also important.

Doty (p. 78) correctly emphasizes that all these techniques (source, form, and redaction criticism) are used to clarify the dynamics at work in the production of the texts we have, not to replace them with some reconstructed earlier source or to discount the importance of authorship. They expose the processes of thought that went into the composition of the scriptural texts.

Documents may be studied for different reasons. If the purpose is proclamation or understanding that teaches modern man, some form of conceptual translation is necessary. But if the purpose is the writing of history, the final critical step is *historical criticism* (Grobel, p. 412) or "attention to the *historical situation*" (Reumann, p. 665). It includes elements from external and internal criticism.

First one finds out all that he can about the author and his situation, for his state of being affects his composition. If the work is anonymous (Hebrews, 1 John), one tries to describe the characteristics of the unknown author. The exact relationship of the author to the document needs to be stated as precisely as possible, since authorship in the ancient world has a much broader spectrum of possibilities.[41] One then carries out

M. Tucker, *Form Criticism of the Old Testament* (Philadelphia: Fortress Press, 1971; Edgar V. McKnight, *What Is Form Criticism?* (Philadelphia: Fortress Press, 1969); Klaus Koch, *The Growth of the Biblical Tradition: The Form-Critical Method* (New York: Charles Scribner's Sons, 1971=1969); Rolf Knierim, "Old Testament Form Criticism Reconsidered," *Interpretation*, 27 (1973): 435–468.

40. Norman Perrin, *What Is Redaction Criticism?* (Philadelphia: Fortress Press, 1969); Walter E. Rast, *Tradition History and the Old Testament* (Philadelphia: Fortress Press, 1972); Joachim Rhode, *Rediscovering the Teaching of the Evangelists* (Philadelphia: Westminster Press, 1969).

41. Raymond Brown, "Canonicity," *The Jerome Biblical Commentary* (Englewood Cliffs, N.J.: Prentice-Hall, 1968), II, 531–532 lists five levels of authorship in antiquity: (1) actual inscription; (2) dictation; (3) supplying of ideas to a "secretary"; (4) composition by a disciple

a similar process for the audience for which the book was written.

One determines the precise literary and conceptual singularity of the book, and its form, intention, and purpose in order to pass judgment on the accuracy and completeness of the historical reports in it. (These first two points are the material of traditional introduction.) One will also seek to locate an author (or book) in the flow or progress of the social, political, or religious history of Israel or the early church (Blank, pp. 37–38); the book must be seen in relation to antecedent and subsequent events.

Since the Bible arose in the Mediterranean world, biblical scholarship also attempts to place the biblical traditions in the broader world of their time, that is in the religious and cultural-political context (Stuhlmacher, p. 39). This procedure describes the cultural and religious terrain in which biblical events happened and the horizon on which biblical authors looked as they wrote. It stresses the ties of biblical literature to its context.

Most descriptions of exegetical method include another step in the process of interpretation (see note 31 above); there is debate as to whether this is a part of historical criticism or a supplement to it. It is related to the historian's aim to understand the past. Scholars describe it in various ways as determining or "formulating the meaning" (Reumann, pp. 666–670), giving a "religious or theological explication" or "a theological or interpretive translation" (Doty, p. 85), an "interpretation" (Stuhlmacher, pp. 39–45), or a "theological-critical interpretation" (Smitmans, pp. 190–193). Some see this step as part of the process of historical criticism (so Stuhlmacher, p. 23) while others view it as a separate procedure that is particularly theological (so Zenger, p. 143, Smitmans, p. 190). German Protestants often formulate this question in terms of the need for *Sachkritik* (content criticism) to evaluate the theological adequacy of an author's statements, and of the need for a canon within the canon from which to survey the whole. Defenders of *Sachkritik* will be noted in chapter five.

We described the virtues of the secular historian as intellectual curiosity, the possession of the necessary knowledge

---

whose ideas are guided by his master's words and spirit; (5) writing in the tradition for which a man was famous, e.g., Moses and law, David and poetry, etc.

requisite to use historical sources, the ability to think critically, a passionate urge for truth, and a basic honesty. These lead to proper balance, humility, and self-criticism. The biblical historian needs them all.

Interpretation of a written text is the reverse of the creative process. The interpreter faces an objective fact, a document. To understand it or to use it to understand the past he must recreate the process of intellectual understanding, creative thought, and composition that went into its production. For all interpreters this process demands certain attitudes. The first is respect for the text that has, as Betti puts it, hermeneutical autonomy.[42] By this phrase Betti means that the interpreter may not import meaning into the text, but must find the sense in the text; the text determines the meaning, not vice versa. This autonomy of the text is the mother of such rules as the need to observe context, the structure of thought, and the coherence of the text. This commonplace has major significance for all understanding of texts. The respect for the texts means that biblical scholarship works in the ancient languages and with as great a knowledge of the surrounding world as possible.[43] The scholar regards textual data as important and seeks to understand them.

The interpreter will also recognize the validity of the "canon of totality" (Betti, p. 15). He will interpret the parts of a document in terms of the whole document, the whole document as part of a larger cultural whole. He will seek a balance between submerging everything in generalities and elevating everything to unique, unparalleled facts.

He will recognize the value of raising questions and putting forth theories, since this process leads to progress in understanding. He will expect his own theories to be criticized by his peers, and will criticize them himself, knowing some of the hypotheses will fall, others will be refined, and a very few will be accepted. In this process he seeks to "preserve the data" (Neill, pp. 336–337; Hanson, pp. 13–15). He will go where the texts lead him. In short, the critical biblical scholar will not only question the texts, but himself—his methods, his conclu-

---

42. Emilio Betti, *Die Hermeneutik als allgemeine Methodik der Geisteswissenschaften* (2. Aufl. Tübingen: J. C. B. Mohr, 1972), p. 14.
43. Rudolf Bultmann, "Is Exegesis without Presuppositions Possible?" *Existence and Faith,* ed. Schubert Ogden (New York: Meridian Books, 1960), p. 291.

sions, and his presuppositions—and the others who share in the same task. For he knows how often men are captive to their own prejudices and limitations, how little each man sees of the whole, how often his historical judgment, imagination, and his ability to synthesize his findings into a coherent whole are less than adequate (Neill, pp. 279, 283–284). To use historical criticism means above all to be critical of one's self.

This criticism is twofold. On the one hand the historian remains critical of his own critical abilities. His work is always *sub iudice*, under his own judgment. But in a more profound sense he recognizes that in judging a text he also places himself under the judgment of the text. And where that text deals with the profundities of man, that calls for a submission to the autonomy of the text that calls the historian forth for judgment and knowledge of himself. Then history performs its humane or (in the case of biblical texts) its theological function.[44]

44. Cf. R. G. Collingwood, *The Idea of History* (New York: Oxford University Press, 1957), *passim*.

IV

Presuppositions and Achievements

Ernst Troeltsch's essay "On Historical and Dogmatic Method in Theology" (1898) formulated the principles of historical criticism.[1] The essay still haunts theology. According to Troeltsch, the historical method of thought and explanation has three principles: (1) the principle of criticism or methodological doubt, which implies that history only achieves probability. Religious tradition must also be subjected to criticism (pp. 731–732). (2) The principle of analogy makes criticism possible. Present experience and occurrence become the criteria of probability in the past. This "almighty power" of analogy implies that all events are in principle similar (p. 732). (3) The principle of correlation (or mutual interdependence) implies that all historical phenomena are so interrelated that a change in one phenomenon necessitates a change in the causes leading to it and in the effects it has (p. 733). Historical explanation rests on this chain of cause and effect. The third principle rules out miracle and salvation history (pp. 740–742). Historical method is the child of the Enlightenment.

But it is inescapable. Admitted at one point, it is a leaven that "changes everything and finally destroys the dogmatic form of method that has been used in theology" (p. 730). Its value is demonstrated by its surprisingly illuminating results. It has two consequences with which theology must come to terms. (1) Criticism makes every individual event uncertain. Only events that stand within a relationship to other events

1. *"Über historische und dogmatische Methode in der Theologie,"* Zur *religiösen Lage, Religionsphilosophie und Ethik* (2. Aufl., *Ges. Schr.* II. Aalen: Scientia Verlag, 1962=1922), pp. 729–753. Troeltsch is discussed by Walter Bodenstein, *Neige zum Historismus* (Gütersloh: Gerd Mohn, 1959) and Van A. Harvey, *The Historian and the Believer* (New York: Macmillan, 1966), pp. 3–6, 14–16.

and have an effect on the present are certain. (2) Christianity loses its uniqueness, for it can be understood only in relation to the whole of history.[2]

Contemporary historians use Troeltsch's three principles, but with significant modifications. Some of their axioms are rarely expressed, but assumed by all. Marc Bloch reminds us that the comparison of accounts rests on the Aristotelian logical principle of contradiction which denies that "an event can both be and not be at the same time."[3] Another often expressed axiom holds that one cannot replace a doubtful transmitted account with one's own guesses.[4] In the case of a gap in the tradition, we can only pronounce a *non liquet* (it is unclear).

It is a basic assumption that the evidence in sources can be recovered by the historian, verified by another researcher, and that history is therefore a controllable discipline. This assumption implies the axiom that all knowledge (or even all truth) is historically conditioned, so that the historical coefficient must at all times be taken into account. This axiom underlies Troeltsch's first principle (criticism), which is thus acknowledged and affirmed by all modern historical study.[5] This assumption allows history to be scientific, for historical knowledge is capable of verification or correction by a reexamination of the evidence.[6] This openness to correction implies that his-

2. F. H. Bradley's essay on the presuppositions of critical history (summarized by Harvey, *The Historian and the Believer*, pp. 70–72) closely parallels Troeltsch's position. This restriction of reality to what can be demonstrated inside the closed continuum of cause and effect by analogical reason is often called historicism. J. H. Hexter, *Doing History* (Bloomington and London: Indiana University Press, 1971), pp. 70–71, argues from the philosopher Carl Hempel that this position is still held by many philosophers, and opposed by historians.

3. *The Historian's Craft* (Manchester: Manchester University Press, 1954), p. 112.

4. Robert Grant, *A Historical Introduction to the New Testament* (London: Collins, 1963), p. 78. The abuse of this axiom does not invalidate it.

5. Josef Blank, "Was bleibt vom Worte Gottes," *Verändert Interpretation den Glauben* (Freiburg: Herder, 1972), p. 33.

6. S. E. Morison, "Faith of a Historian," *American Historical Review*, 56 (1951): 290; Jürgen Moltmann, "Exegese und Eschatologie der Geschichte," *Perspektiven der Theologie* (München: Chr. Kaiser Verlag, 1968), pp. 62–64; Rudolf Bultmann, "Is Exegesis without presuppositions possible?" *Existence and Faith*, ed. Schubert M. Ogden (New York: Meridian Books, 1960), p. 290.

torical research produces only probabilities, a conclusion which raises questions about the certainty of faith and its object in theology.

All historians also accept Troeltsch's principle of analogy. We are able to restore the past, as Bloch puts it (p. 44), only by borrowing from the present and shading it. The axiom is that nature, society, and man possess a certain uniformity that prevents too great deviations and so makes meaningful assertion possible (Harvey, p. 98). Bloch (pp. 115–116) limits this uniformity to "some very general characteristics" that allow for infinite variation. A problem arises when this uniformity is raised to a universal principle that makes some evidence inadmissible. History works with principles that allow for verification. Its grounds for belief must be clear. They extend from common sense and truisms, through epigraphic or archaeological or topographical data, to scientific principles and logical argumentation.[7] An overgeneralization of a warrant leads to a constriction of the historian's viewpoint so that it is no longer possible to encompass all of reality.

Troeltsch's third principle, correlation, is a good illustration of the complexity of historical explanation via general principles. All historians accept the principle of causation as an axiom to be used in historical explanation.[8] Causation is more complex than one may assume. Every event has a number of causes. The historian presupposes that these causes can be identified, exhibited and interrelated so that history can be explicated. There are many conceivable causes for Jesus' crucifixion: his decision to go to Jerusalem, the betrayal by Judas, the animosity of the religious establishment for a popular folk-preacher, a weak Roman procurator, the threat of a political uprising around a Galilean revolutionary, the intention of Jesus to offer himself as a sacrifice for the people, the soldiers assigned to the crucifixion detail, the eschatological plan of God, the accident of being in the wrong place when a political scapegoat was needed. The historian selects from these causes those that are not accidental, that are close to the event, that could have been avoided, that are most specific, and yet can be

7. The discussion of warrants and historical evidence is an outstanding contribution of Harvey's book; see *The Historian and the Believer*, pp. 43–64.

8. Bloch, *The Historian's Craft*, pp. 190–192; E. H. Carr, *What Is History?* (Harmondsworth: Penguin Books, 1964), pp. 87–108.

generalized to provide explanation and guidance (Bloch, pp. 190–192; Carr, pp. 102–107).

The historian's interpretation of the past determines which causes he allows and uses to build up a pattern. An argument arises when one asks what type of causation is admissible in history. Bultmann (pp. 291–292) argued that history is "a closed continuum . . . of cause and effect" in which explanation must take place in terms of modern ideas of causation. The validity of the opinion depends upon whether the historian and his audience agree that only sociological, psychological, economic, political, and scientific causation are valid, or agree to allow a theological or transcendental explanation of cause.

The view of history that allows only causation that is not theological or transcendental is historicism. The model for historicism's view of method and truth came from natural science. It looked for reporting in a strictly denotative language that would be clear and unambiguous. Such language is aided by an appeal to general laws. Historicism looked for such types of explanation as would allow for a repetition of the process leading to the conclusion, i.e., a type of explanation modeled on experimental science. It tried to formulate its insights in terms of general laws in such a way "that the event is entailed by the laws through strict deduction."[9] Such laws should give history coherence and aid in the arrival at absolute certainties (Bloch, p. 14). The historicist view, modeled on the laws of natural science, expresses itself in the exclusion of God as a causative factor and in the denial of the possibility of miracle.[10]

Historicism provided valuable contributions to historical work. It made a virtue of careful, meticulous attention to detail as part of the concern for veracity and verification. It emphasized careful analysis and the precise formulation of problems and conclusions. That legacy should never be lost. Historicism also led to the belief that the historian himself did not produce the conclusions which were inherent in the data. Rather, the historian felt he uncovered the principles and laws that work in history so that prediction and instruction can come from his-

9. The description is taken from Hexter, pp. 28–30, 67–70. Hexter, *Doing History*, is reporting the view of the analytical philosopher Carl Hempel, "Function of General Laws in History," *Journal of Philosophy*, 41 (1943): 35–48.

10. Cf. Carl Braaten, *History and Hermeneutic* (Philadelphia: Westminster Press, 1966), pp. 18–20, 36–38. In the late nineteenth and early twentieth centuries this was combined with evolutionary optimism.

tory (Hexter, pp. 139–140; Bloch, pp. 14–16; Carr, pp. 57–60).

It is a truism today to assert that historical research is no longer historicistic or positivistic. There is a changed climate in science and history that no longer is as certain of the universality and immutability of laws. Bloch (p. 17) argues that science has substituted the idea of the *infinitely probable* for the certain. The generalizations that are made are called "statements of tendency" of "general propositions" and serve as hypotheses to enable further thought, refinement, modification, or refutation. The historian has been influenced by this development and freed from the idea of laws in history. The historian sets himself the task of explaining the past in terms of the forces that made it happen as it did.[11]

If the concept of law is no longer so rigidly observed in secular historiography, this does not mean that a theological interpretation of history is more respectable. Carr, for example, rules out the possibility of interference of "some super-historical force" in any form ("the God of a Chosen People, a Christian God, the Hidden Hand of the Deist, or Hegel's World Spirit"). Divine interference in history is a *deus ex machina* explanation for Carr, a joker in the deck that is not compatible with the integrity of history as the study of man (p. 75). Harvey holds that faith in some kind of divine interference has a falsifying effect, because it is really special pleading for the Christian position that assumes what needs to be proved (pp. 107–115). It is only an extension of the same principle to deny the possibility of miracle. Miracle, the overt intrusion of God into history, destroys the neutrality that is required for the historian's work.[12] Harvey states that miracle cannot be ruled out as a logical possibility; but "nothing can be said in [its] favor and a great deal counts against it" (p. 86). Present experience

11. This change in climate has also highlighted the role of the scholar in the process of generalization. He selects the relevant materials, forms the pattern, and thus imposes meaning on his material. This view of the historian, states Carr, makes a historicist theory of objective knowledge incompatible with the nature of history. Objectivity is not determined by dispassionate observation, but by the standard of significance. The objective historian is the one who finds the materials necessary to the end in view and represents them without distortion (Carr, *What Is History?* pp. 70–73; Morison, "Faith of a Historian," p. 264). The wall between the historian and his object is gone.

12. So Robert Morgan, *The Nature of New Testament Theology* (London: SCM Press, 1973), p. 21, with references to Wrede and Troeltsch.

does not allow an analogical argument for miracle except in cases where contemporary thought is not certain of its knowledge (e.g., psychosomatic healings, healing miracles). In such a case an historian will not feel justified in ruling out a very strange possibility, because the warrants or contemporary knowledge are less compelling (p. 116). Historians recognize that there are causes they cannot fit into their rational patterns (coincidence, Bloch, pp. 130–132; accident, Carr, pp. 102–104), reality that will not fit their categories. But they do not bring these irrational causes into any discussion of a theonomous view of history. Bultmann's view is more carefully stated, for while he affirms the closed cause and effect continuum, he also says that historical scholarship "may not assert that such a faith is an illusion and that God has not acted in history" (p. 292).

J. H. Hexter argues that three great changes have affected historians in recent years. (1) They have been freed from the "stultifying effect of the positivist rules of historical method." Historians theorize with better consciences, for they now know clearly that explanation is imposed by the historian and is not in the facts themselves. (2) The historian has been freed also from substantive philosophies of history such as logical positivism and analytic philosophy. Hexter passes a devastating judgment on their value for history:

Intelligent criticism has reduced both positivism and the substantive philosophy of history to methodological absurdity, equally futile and preposterous modes of dealing with the data available to historians, chimeras to which no historian need pay heed, except insofar as he happens to be interested in the history of systematic intellectual error of a sort similar to astrology, heptascopy and phrenology. (p. 140)

History has its own form of explanation, narrative that is not captive to analogy. (3) Secular history no longer assumes the function of providing guidance for the solution of the world's ills. It has been dethroned from its nineteenth-century position to serve the more modest goal of understanding and explaining the past (Hexter, pp. 139–142; 69–76).

Hexter's views stand in sharp contrast to those of Harvey, who uses recent linguistic philosophers as his reference point in evaluating biblical scholarship. Hexter insists that the methods, warrants, and form of history must grow out of the need to maximize the communication of historical knowledge and truth. His formulation is open. Harvey's use of warrants assumes a closed universe; it does not leave room for divine action in history. His view precludes the possibility that the Bible's own view of history could be true. But Hexter's description of historical narrative leaves room for the theological claim of the Bible. Historical method is anything but a carefully defined and agreed on set of axioms and presuppositions.

THE BASIS FOR HISTORICAL CRITICISM IN THEOLOGY

Theology cannot return to a precritical age; this is the common view in current exegetical literature (Blank, p. 34, and many others). Christian theologians may greet the acceptance of historical methods as "one of the great events in the history of Christianity"[13] or long for the simpler past, but they can in the present only seek to use historical criticism in the service of the Gospel. Historical method is in its general axioms at best not hostile to theology, at worst a threat to the central message of the Scripture. Theology must either justify the use of historical criticism and define its nature or be willing to reformulate the Christian faith in terms of a positivist truth that historicism alone will validate. Most theologians argue that the former course is open and give a theological justification for historical criticism.[14]

Historical criticism is not a threat to the Scriptures because it is congruent with its object, the Bible. The Bible is an ancient book addressed to people of long ago in a strange culture, written in ancient languages. Historical criticism respects this historical gap and uses a method to determine as precisely as possible the significance of the words for the people then. Historical criticism sets the Bible squarely into our history and makes the "full brightness and impact of Christian ideas" shine out.[15] Historical interpretation does this task best.

13. Paul Tillich, *Systematic Theology* (Chicago: University of Chicago Press, 1957), II, 107.
14. Van Harvey seems to take the latter course, redefining the content of Christianity as "some insight into the nature of reality itself" in its bearing on "the human quest for liberation and fulfillment" (*The Historian and the Believer*, p. 258).
15. W. C. van Unnik, "ἡ καινὴ διαθήκη—A Problem in the Early History of the Canon," *Studia Patristica* (Berlin: Akademie Verlag, 1961), IV, 217.

The Bible's time-conditioned words speak to specific situations in the literary conventions and forms of their day. They have the appearance of the accidental because they are written *more humano et historico* (in a human and historically conditioned manner).[16] As the ancient dogmatic formula put it, the scriptures are *panta anthrôpina*, completely human. This basic recognition about the nature of the Bible entails the axiom that one interprets the Bible by the same methods and procedures used on any other book. No serious Bible student denies this evaluation.

The old dogmatic formula continued that the Bible is also *panta theia*, completely divine. The emphasis on the historical side of the Bible leads to various formulations about the Word of God and the Bible. "Certainly, for all Christian Churches, the Word of God and the canon belong together. But they are in no way identical, as orthodoxy would have it."[17] Josef Blank (pp. 46–49) speaks more cautiously of the Bible as witness to Word of God from beginning to end. It is clear that the old formula written in ontological terms is strongly challenged by historical information.

Cullman stresses that the central affirmation of the Bible, "Jesus is Christ the Lord," has to do with history.[18] The Bible narrates that history. As an historical document the Bible lies open to historical investigation. Such investigation does not demonstrate a lack of faith. Rather it would be unfaith, a denial of the history in the Bible, to refuse to use historical study.[19]

16. The phrase "appearance of the accidental" is Walter Kreck's, "Die Gemeinde braucht die Kritik an der Bibel," *Bibelkritik und Gemeindefrömmigkeit*, ed. Hans Dieter Bastian (Gütersloh: Gerd Mohn, 1966), pp. 50–52. Roman Catholic scholarship has emphasized this point: Blank, "Was bleibt vom Worte Gottes," p. 29: Josef Ernst, "Das hermeneutische Problem im Wandel der Auslegungsgeschichte," *Schriftauslegung* (München, Paderborn, Wien: Verlag Friedrich Schöningh, 1972), pp. 49–50.
17. Ernst Käsemann, "Thoughts on the Present Controversy about Scriptural Interpretation," *New Testament Questions of Today*, trans. W. J. Montague (Philadelphia: Fortress Press, 1969), p. 263. Erich Dinkler, "Bibelkritik," *Die Religion in der Geschichte und Gegenwart* (3 Aufl. Tübingen: J. C. B. Mohr, 1957), I, 1189, says the Word of God is present in the Bible *in actu*, but not ontologically.
18. Oscar Cullmann, "The Necessity and Function of Higher Criticism," *The Early Church*, ed. A. J. B. Higgins (Philadelphia: Westminster Press, 1956), p. 7.
19. Karl Hermann Schelkle, "Sacred Scripture and the Word of God," *Dogmatic Versus Biblical Theology* (Baltimore: Helicon, 1968), p. 17.

Historical criticism is used because the Bible gives a witness to an historical event; it raises a claim to historical *truth*.[20] To refuse to use historical criticism in the face of the Bible's claim would deny that the history told is true history, make impossible intellectual demands on faith, and separate history from the Bible that stresses its importance. It would be a form of the docetic heresy.

Finally, the Bible is not an esoteric book of some secret society, but a word that presses for proclamation to the world. Proclamation demands translation into the language of the people. Translation is best done through a method that identifies the ancient message precisely and aids in the translation. Biblical criticism done for this purpose is a mark of "deepest respect before the Word of God" (Kreck, p. 54) and opens up the possibilities for contemporary proclamation.[21]

BY THEIR FRUITS SHALL YE KNOW THEM

Historical criticism is ultimately judged by its results and utility; the results are an immense validation for the use of the method.

(1) Critical scholars have provided the *research tools* in use today, from grammars, lexica, and concordances, through critical text editions, to the great theological dictionaries, commentaries, and histories that are the staple fare of every exegete. All translations of the Bible in use today rest on such tools and are the result of such historical work. Critical scholars have pioneered all the methods in use: scientific methods of archaeology, form and redaction criticism, etc. In spite of blind alleys and false starts tools and methods have been developed and refined to a high level. The style for biblical scholarship has been set by critical scholarship.[22]

(2) Through the study of the *geographical* and *historical*

Kurt Frör, *Biblische Hermeneutik* (München: Chr. Kaiser Verlag, 1961), pp. 48–49, makes the same point.
20. Arnold A. T. Ehrhardt, "The Theology of New Testament Criticism," *The Framework of the New Testament Stories* (Cambridge: Harvard University Press, 1964), p. 3.
21. Gerhard Ebeling, *The Problem of Historicity in the Church and Its Proclamation*, trans. Grover Foley (Philadelphia: Fortress Press, 1967), pp. 15–24.
22. G. Eldon Ladd has pointed this out to fellow evangelicals in no uncertain terms, *The New Testament and Criticism* (Grand Rapids: Wm. B. Eerdmans, 1967), pp. 10–11.

context the life and history of Israel and the early church have been given new light. The ancient Near Eastern and Graeco-Roman cultures have been clarified through archaeology, social-economic history, and cultural history. The nature of slavery, the character of law, the significance of household gods, Rabbinic traditions, synagogue architecture, ecstatic prophecy, the Roman road system, and a host of other details are known better by us than they have been known for a millennium and more. And if the fragile society we live in endures and such investigation continues, our children and grandchildren may smile at our naiveté.

(3) We have a better grasp of the original grammatical and *historical sense* of the Bible, which the Reformers praised so highly (the *unus simplex sensus,* the *sensus historicus sive grammaticus*). One cannot overpraise this achievement. The course of biblical history has been clarified at many points. We see the concerns and objectives, the conflicting claims and loyalties, the bitter struggles and failures of Israel and the church with greater clarity. We also recognize the gaps in our knowledge more clearly—and that is significant progress. The history of Syrian Christianity from A.D. 30 to 100 is dark, and Alexandria (Egypt) is in this period a closed book. The mark of the true historian is his willingness to pronounce his *ignosco* (I don't know).[23]

(4) The *time-conditioned, historical character* of the Bible has been made evident. This insight enables us to understand problem areas (e.g., the imprecatory psalms) more sympathetically. The continuity of the biblical revelation with our time has been stressed; an unwitting docetic view of the Bible is made difficult.[24]

(5) Historical criticism puts us into the place of Jesus' first hearers by making the Bible seem *strange and foreign.* Palestine is an earthy place; Israel's prophets and Jesus do not

23. See Ferdinand Hahn, "Probleme historischer Kritik," *Zeitschrift für die neutestamentliche Wissenschaft,* 63 (1972): 9; John Knox, *Criticism and Faith* (New York, Nashville: Abingdon Press, 1952), pp. 79–88; Peter Stuhlmacher, "Zur Methoden-und Sachproblematik einer interkonfessionellen Auslegung des Neuen Testaments," *Evangelisch-Katholischer Kommentar zum Neuen Testament. Vorarbeiten,* Heft 4 (Zürich, Einsiedeln, Köln: Benziger Verlag; Neukirchen: Neukirchener Verlag, 1972), p. 39.
24. James Smart, *The Strange Silence of the Bible in the Church* (Philadelphia: Westminster Press, 1970), pp. 82–83. This point is a *Leitmotif* in Ernst Käsemann's writings.

resemble the well-laundered pictures of them prevalent in much piety and art. Historical criticism makes the gap between us and the biblical world as wide as it actually is, forces us to face the peculiarity and particularity of the texts in their world, and confronts us with the Jesus who is the challenge to all cultures and securities of our world. Historical study prevents too rapid modernizing.[25]

(6) Historical criticism provides a way for the Scriptures to exercise their *proper critical function* in the church. Historical criticism is tied to the texts, not to modern concerns or problems and so leaves the texts their integrity.[26] It seeks to hear the texts *de novo*, without the weight of the dogmatic tradition and church history interfering (Hahn, pp. 8–9; Grant, p. 87). This reduces the subjective element in interpretation by helping to select the true meaning from the possible meanings.[27] An illustration may clarify. In Matt. 11:28–30 Jesus issues the invitation: "Come to me, all who labor and are heavy-laden, and I will give you rest. Take my yoke upon you and learn from me; for I am gentle and lowly in heart, and you will find rest for your souls. For my yoke is easy, and my burden is light" (RSV). These verses have been used to encourage the oppressed, the weary, the overburdened housewife, and those who worry too much. Historical criticism makes clear that these words of Jesus are spoken in opposition to the demand for the taking up of the "yoke of the Torah"; Jesus rather offers the free gift of the rule of God. (Cf. Sirach 51:23ff., the counterpoise to Jesus' words.) The passage is properly used to comfort those who are oppressed by the burden of responsibility for their own well-being before God.

25. Robert Funk, "The Hermeneutical Problem and Historical Criticism," *The New Hermeneutic* (New York and Evanston: Harper & Row, 1964), pp. 183–184; Kreck, "Die Gemeinde braucht die Kritik an der Bibel," pp. 59–60.
26. Smart, *Strange Silence,* p. 80; Cullmann, "Higher Criticism," pp. 15–16. Adolf Schlatter saw this clearly: "Our work has a historical purpose when it is not concerned with the interests which emerge from the course of our own life, but directs its attention quite deliberately away from ourselves and our own contemporary interests, back to the past." "The Theology of the New Testament and Dogmatics," *The Nature of New Testament Theology,* ed. Robert Morgan (London: SCM Press, 1973), p. 118.
27. So Cullmann, "Higher Criticism," pp. 15–16; Alan Richardson, "The Rise of Modern Biblical Scholarship and Recent Discussion of the Authority of the Bible," *The Cambridge History of the Bible,* vol. III: *The West from the Reformation to the Present Day* (Cambridge: at the University Press, 1963), p. 302, illustrates how a literalist interpretation of Ex. 22:18 led to witch burnings.

(7) Historical criticism is *self-correcting*. Arbitrary reconstructions and wild theories are doomed to rejection by scholars who measure them against the texts. Texts are uncompromising masters who drive out bad criticism by calling forth better evaluations. The history of criticism shows how the process of correction goes on. *Abusus non tollit usum* (misuse does not destroy proper use).[28]

(8) Historical criticism has effected significant change in *theological insight*. The meticulous investigation of the biblical texts has brought to light the magnificent variety in the Bible. It has forced theology to rethink the nature of the Scriptures in the light of that variety and the human, time-conditioned factor that it highlights. Scholars find the unity of the Scriptures either in the unity of God (Schelkle, p. 16) or the history of salvation (Richardson, p. 299).

(9) The emphasis on history has affected every branch of theology. *Theological method* has been *altered*, as Troeltsch said it would—but not in the manner he expected. The different theological disciplines today recognize that the Bible must be read historically and then interpreted for our own age. To detach the Bible's contents from history is to deny the very nature of the Scriptures and the Gospel they proclaim (Knox, pp. 91–92; Richardson, p. 300). The theological disciplines have also reminded historical criticism of its limitations. Its results tell us what proclamation was in Israel and in the primitive church at a particular time and place. But it does not tell us what the form of proclamation should be today. It makes clear what factors and elements constituted the early proclamation, and thereby indicates the need for systematic and practical theology in our time.[29]

28. Erich Dinkler, "Bibelautorität und Bibelkritik," *Signum Crucis* (Tübingen: J. C. B. Mohr, 1967), pp. 190–191; Günther Bornkamm, "Die ökumenische Bedeutung der historisch-kritischen Bibelwissenschaft," *Geschichte und Glaube,* Band II (München: Chr. Kaiser Verlag, 1971), pp. 13–14.
29. Trutz Rendtorff, "Historische Bibelwissenschaft und Theologie," *Theorie des Christentums* (Gütersloh: Gerd Mohn, 1972), pp. 51–57. Roy Harrisville, *His Hidden Grace* (Nashville, New York: Abingdon Press, 1965), pp. 58–59, comments strikingly that moving from Palestine to our world is "the hardest, the bitterest of them all, and the question as to the proper balance between this actualizing and the steps which precede it will occupy biblical critics, pastors, and teachers long after we have turned to sod." John Reumann, "Methods in Studying the Biblical Text Today," *Concordia Theological Monthly,* 40 (1969): 666–670, suggests a process for actualization.

(10) Historical criticism produces only probable results. It relativizes everything. But faith needs certainty. Uneasy Christians ask whether those who make the historical confession that Jesus died under Pontius Pilate and rose again the third day can be content with mere probability. Defenders of historical criticism point out that the probability factor is actually a virtue. It removes the idolatry that confuses the temporal and the eternal (Smart, p. 84) and points out the true nature of faith (Harrisville, pp. 78–80). Historicism has falsely taught that one should accept as true and believe only what can be established by positivist, rational proofs. But the believing critic knows "that there is truth which must not be demonstrated by historical proofs," for then it disappears.[30] Criticism frees us from the tyranny of history and makes the vulnerability of faith clear. It makes us hear the biblical proclamation as the first Christians did—without any security outside of the proclamation that confronts us with its demand for believing response—and this alone gives certainty to faith.[31]

OBJECTIONS AND MODIFICATIONS

The contributions of historical critical inquiry have not blinded scholars to the problems that historical criticism poses for theology. Does it adequately evaluate the Scriptures, the normative text of the Christian faith? Is the historical method used by an interpreter of the Bible the same as the method used on other documents, if the interpreter's faith determines his attitude to the Bible? If it is, is it not inadequate and destructive? How must it be modified to measure up to its object? Scholars have recently struggled to answer these and similar weighty questions.

(1) The objection is made that the historian's methods are secular and profane and so will destroy faith by shaking the old traditions, the landmarks of the faith (so formulated by Bornkamm, p. 14). Biblical scholarship should reject such a secular and destructive mode of inquiry. It is true that historical inquiry has at times been destructive. But so has every

30. Eduard Schweizer, "Die historisch-kritische Bibelwissenschaft und die Verkündigungsaufgabe der Kirche," *Neotestamentica* (Zürich /Stuttgart: Calwer Verlag, 1963), pp. 139–142.
31. Julius Schniewind, "Gewissheit—nicht Sicherheit," *Zur Erneuerung des Christenstandes,* ed. Hans Joachim Kraus (Göttingen: Vandenhoeck & Ruprecht, 1966), pp. 33–43, distinguishes certainty from security. Cf. Dinkler, *Bibelautorität,* p. 195.

other method ever used in the history of the church, historical criticism has not had a corner on heresy. It is also a mistake to think that there is such a thing as a sacred method. A method does not have faith or unbelief; there are only believing or unbelieving interpreters. As little as there are sacred engineering and architecture used in the construction of a church building, so little is there a sacred method of interpreting a text.[32]

(2) The problem can be reformulated. Faith and historical method have two different means of determining truth and reality. The secular method of historical criticism will lead the Christian into intellectual dualism, for history and faith have separate and distinct warrants; the Christian who uses historical methods must live in two worlds that clash.[33] Christians have lived with this problem for centuries. Solutions are offered in various ways. Barth, for example, relegated historical interpretation to a preliminary stage, important, but subordinated to theological or dialectical exegesis. The dualism was overcome by making historical interpretation theologically irrelevant. Bultmann solved the problem by making the theological function of historical criticism the demonstration that man's historicality lies in his need for authentic existence. The address of the kerygma in the Scriptures calls him to that existence, and his response is faith. The dualism is solved by a redefinition of history in existentialist and anthropological terms. Bultmann has been faulted for making the question "What really happened?" irrelevant and thus actually denigrating history.

(3) In recent years the integration of faith and historical method has been accomplished by challenging the adequacy of historical method's positivist axioms. God and history are not exclusive alternatives. Biblical criticism therefore has to challenge a view of reality that operates with a closed universe and an absolutely naturalist ontology.[34] Historicist axioms do not measure up to the claim of the Scriptures that "God does

32. Dinkler, *Bibelautorität*, pp. 202–203 (above, note 28).
33. Frör, *Biblische Hermeneutik*, pp. 56–60 and Martin Franzmann, "The Hermeneutical Dilemma: Dualism in the Interpretation of Holy Scripture," *Concordia Theological Monthly*, 36 (1965): 502–533, make similar analyses. Cf. also Braaten, *History and Hermeneutik*, pp. 36–37.
34. The argumentation is Paul Minear's, "Gospel History: Celebration or Reconstruction?" *Jesus and Man's Hope*, ed. Donald G. Miller and Dikran Y. Hadidian (Pittsburgh: Pittsburgh Theological Seminary, 1971), II, 23.

his work of grace and judgment not outside man and so, too, not beyond history, but in it and through it" (Schlatter, p. 152). History deals with "What really happened"; therefore history needs faith, as faith needs history. Theology presupposes a true act of salvation as a *petitio principii*, and argues that every theological investigation of history must do so also.[35] Some theologians therefore ask historians to stay away from the realm of philosophy and leave an open door for the possibility of divine action in history;[36] it is probably more realistic to ask that historians be as critical of philosophical assumptions as they are of theological ones.

(4). History then must be redefined to allow the possibility of that divine action. This demand is raised by many critical exegetes. The biblical view of God maintains that he works in the present as the God who calls the dead to life (Rom. 4:17) and does wonders (Ps. 77:14). Historical explanation must recognize that God's action has as much claim to serious attention in explanation as do naturalist explanations.[37] It provides structure and coherence. Blank supports this position by pointing to the future direction of biblical history. It contains promise, and so is not passé but relevant to the present. Historians struggle to find a way to relate their research to the present. Biblical insights may point the way.[38]

(5). The modification in the definition of history that is proposed also has an effect on the warrants that are used in historical work. Recent debate has circled around the historicity of the resurrection of Jesus. Biblical scholars refuse to allow analogical reason from present experience to rule out the possibility of the resurrection. They disagree as to whether historical evidence can be used to compel the historian (logically, *qua* historian) to accept the resurrection as a unique event,[39] or

35. Hans Grass, "Historisch-kritische Forschung und Dogmatik," *Theologie und Kritik* (Göttingen: Vandenhoeck & Ruprecht, 1969), p. 26; cf. Ladd, *The New Testament and Criticism*, p. 33.

36. Smart, *Strange Silence*, p. 110; Stephen Neill, *The Interpretation of the New Testament 1861–1961* (London: Oxford University Press, 1966), pp. 279–281.

37. Alan Richardson, *The Bible in the Age of Science* (London: SCM Press, 1961), pp. 127–131; Grass, "Historisch-kritische Forschung und Dogmatik," pp. 19–22.

38. Josef Blank, "Die Interpretation der Bibel als theologisches Problem," *Schriftauslegung in Theorie und Praxis* (München: Kösel Verlag, 1969), pp. 24–29.

whether it can only argue that some decisive event took place, to which faith adds that the resurrection provides an adequate explanation (Harrisville, pp. 74–78). In both cases, however, the historicist assumption that the unique is impossible is rejected. In principle, therefore, the possibility of miracle is allowed, although each miracle reported in the Bible is judged on the basis of the evidence presented (Dinkler, *Bibelautorität*, p. 194).

(6) Faith has clearly become a factor in historical critical work by (some) biblical scholars. Does this mean the biblical critic is not objective? The biblical critic means to hear the texts on their terms. He comes to the texts without having decided in advance what they mean or say. He is objective in that sense.[40] Such objectivity does not mean that the interpreter is removed from the process of interpretation. Objectivity is rather the recognition of personal involvement and taking it into account in interpretation.[41]

(7) Objectivity does not demand neutrality or freedom from presuppositions. Emilio Betti (pp. 53–57) lays down the principle that the mind-set of the interpreter must correspond to the object being interpreted as a canon of interpretation. Bultmann (pp. 292–295) speaks of a "life relation" to the subject matter. The biblical interpreter comes to the Bible presuming that his texts have something valid to say that he does not already know and that what they say will relate to the judging and saving word of God (Frör, pp. 53–54). He stands in the succession of those who have heard the Scripture and been imprinted by the history of its interpretation.[42] There is thus a movement from the text to the interpreter and then back to the text (the hermeneutical circle). Theologically this means that the role of the Holy Spirit in interpretation may be taken seriously.

40. So Albrecht Oepke, *Geschichtliche und übergeschichtliche Schriftauslegung* (2. Aufl. Gütersloh: C. Bertelsman, 1947), pp. 17–19; Blank, *Verändert*, p. 32.
41. See Rudolf Schnackenburg, "Zur Auslegung der Heiligen Schrift in unserer Zeit," *Bibel und Leben*, 5 (1964): 221–222; Louis Alonzo Schökel, "Hermeneutics in the Light of Language and Literature," *Catholic Biblical Quarterly*, 25 (1963): 381; Emilio Betti, *Die Hermeneutik als allgemeine Methodik der Geistes-Wissenschaften* (2. Aufl. Tübingen: J. C. B. Mohr, 1972), p. 27.
42. Erich Dinkler, "Das Wort Gottes, die Bible und die wissenschaftliche Methode," *Fragen der wissenschaftlichen Erforschung der Heiligen Schrift*, Sonderdruck aus dem Protokoll der Landessynode der Evangelischen Kirche im Rheinland (January, 1962), p. 8.

(8) Certain problems are admittedly unresolved. One is the role of *Sachkritik* in historical criticism. *Sachkritik* (content criticism) is the evaluation of the adequacy of what an author says when measured by the criterion of the central affirmation which he (or the entire Bible) makes. It also asks if an author actually says what he meant according to the criterion of internal consistency.[43] The procedure is characteristic of Rudolf Bultmann's pupils. Ebeling and Käsemann especially argue for its necessity; both maintain that it continues the thrust of the Reformation's *sola scriptura*.[44] The question is whether such *Sachkritik* is an intrinsic part of historical criticism, or whether it contradicts the basic intention of the method to leave the texts their integrity, since it is ultimately a means of controlling or even supressing a part of the text.[45]

(9) Another problem is the tendency to exalt historical criticism as the only legitimate way to read the Bible. The result is that the Bible becomes a specialist's book and is no longer the treasure of the church. The hubris of this claim is demonstrated by the experience of countless contemporary Christians and the long experience of the church in reading the Bible in a different manner. We need an analysis of other methods of reading the Bible. It should include the psychological approach, structuralism, and the techniques of literary history. Literary history concentrates on the actual work of literature as an entity in itself. It uses historical criticism for preliminary orientation, but explains literature by an analysis of stylistics, type of discourse, and the life of the literary text after it leaves its author's hand.[46] (Literary criticism and history of literature might be better terms to describe this approach, to distinguish it from form, tradition, and redaction criticism.) A literary document or public document differs from an historical event, for it has an ongoing life in the present. That life

---

43. William Doty, *Contemporary New Testament Interpretation* (Englewood Cliffs, N.J.: Prentice Hall, 1972), p. 21. He credits Bultmann with originating the term.

44. Ebeling, *Problem of Historicity*, pp. 64–66; *Significance*, pp. 42–43; Erst Käsemann, "Vom theologischen Recht historisch-kritischer Exegese," *Zeitschrift für Theologie und Kirche*, 46 (1967): 275 ff.

45. Robert Morgan's argument, *The Nature of New Testament Theology*, pp. 42–50.

46. Schökel, "Hermeneutics in the Light of Language and Literature," p. 385, called for this a decade ago. The techniques of such analysis are described in René Wellek and Austin Warren, *Theory of Literature* (Harmondsworth: Penguin Books, 1973), *passim*.

becomes a part of it, even one of the norms for understanding it (Wellek and Warren, pp. 154–157.). This emphasis reminds one that he cannot read a work of literature as its first readers did; intervening history makes that impossible, at least in part.

(10) Historical research objectifies; to use Betti's phrase, it is contemplative (p. 49). But theology (like law) reads its normative text in order to make an application or concretization for the present (at least in part). The Bible narrates history for a kerygmatic (or edificatory, or doxological) purpose. The correlation of the contemplative objectification of history with the kerygmatic thrust of the Scriptures is an unfinished task.[47] The result is that the Bible is no longer revelation for many who ask how an historically understood Bible can still be used as the Scripture of the church. In what way can a document that is a source for a particular past history be read in worship as Holy Scripture and preached?[48] Exegetical scholars are agreed only that historical criticism, the best method of discovering the literal sense, cannot be given up.

Historical criticism in the service of the Gospel and the mission of the church is the ecclesiastical ideal. Historical criticism in the service of verifiable fact placed into a significant narrative is the historian's ideal. The possible conflict between these two ideals can be resolved only in the person of the interpreter living in the community of faith, who combines dedication to historical truth with the recognition of his own humanity and need for forgiveness. Historical research, like all of man's efforts, is also perverted by sin.[49] But in the community of scholarship that lives in the fellowship of the people of God, the errors that arise from human frailty can be corrected and sin forgiven by God's grace. Then biblical criticism will grow together with faith into the full measure of the stature of Christ, his Gospel, his Word, and his Holy Scripture.

47. This common theme in current exegetical literature is sharply stated by Hahn, "Probleme historischer Kritik," pp. 11–12. See also Schelkle, "Sacred Scripture," pp. 28–29; Schnackenburg, "Zur Auslegung der Heiligen Schrift," p. 221; Smart, *Strange Silence*, p. 33.
48. So formulated by Ulrich Wilckens, "Über die Bedeutung historischer Kritik in der modernen Bibelexegese," *Was heisst Auslegung der Heiligen Schrift?* (Regensburg: Friedrich Pustet, 1966), pp. 87–88. Similar formulations in Dinkler, *Bibelautorität*, p. 180; Smart, *Strange Silence*, pp. 90–93; Blank, *Interpretation*, p. 15; James Muilenburg, "Preface to Hermeneutics," *Journal of Biblical Literature*, 77 (1958): 19–22.
49. See Nels F. S. Ferre, "Notes by a Theologian on Biblical Hermeneutics," *Journal of Biblical Literature*, 78 (1959): 109.

V

Historical Criticism in Theological Discussion since 1945

Discussion of the value and weakness of historical criticism continues in theological literature. In the generation since the end of World War II there was a theological defense of historical criticism in arguments against attacks from more conservative Christians. In this chapter we will trace that debate by summarizing some representative evaluations of historical criticism made from different perspectives.

HISTORICAL CRITICISM AS REFORMATION THEOLOGY

Gerhard Ebeling relates the use of historical critical method to the *sola fide* of Reformation theology and defends it with almost confessional fervor in "The Significance of the Critical Historical Method for Church and Theology" (1950).[1] The Reformers left Protestantism a legacy in which the "Word of God must be left free to assert itself . . . against distortions and fixations." The Reformers were also critical of tradition and held that theology must be left free to translate the Bible into whatever language is required at the moment. This attitude results from the combination of the distinction between law and Gospel and the insistence of the Reformation that Jesus is the Word of God. Together these two insights formed a critical canon within the canon. The Gospel is actualized in the present through the Word of promise received *sola fide*.

The decision in the nineteenth century to use historical criticism "maintained and confirmed over against Roman Catholicism in a different situation the decision of the Reformers in

---

1. *Word and Faith*, trans. James H. Leitch (Philadelphia: Fortress Press, 1963), pp. 17–61.

the sixteenth century." The critical historical method has dangers, e.g., boundless relativism and scientific objectivism. There are, nevertheless, "essential inner connections" between the Reformation and critical historical theology, for the *Sachkritik* of historical criticism has affinities to the Reformation's canon within the canon. Critical historical theology does not disturb true faith, for faith is response to the promise, not acceptance of historical data. Indeed, critical historical theology supports the *sola fide* of the reformers, for it shows faith what its true object is. Therefore, "critical historical theology . . . is the indispensable means of reminding the church of the freedom rooted in the *iustificatio impii*" (p. 60). Ebeling thus responded to his own statement that a new attempt to think through the theological relevance of the critical historical method was a need in theology.[2]

Carl Braaten has criticized Ebeling for using historical criticism basically as law and thus perpetuating the divorce of faith from history.[3] Ebeling makes history irrelevant because his concept of faith is fundamentally that of existentialism. Then, argues Braaten, faith is no longer that of Reformation Christianity, for there faith also had a content.

Ernst Käsemann also has argued that historical criticism has a theological basis. The last of a series of articles appeared in 1967.[4] Käsemann's point of departure is the distinction between the Gospel and Scripture. The canon and the Word belong together, but cannot be identified. The Bible has authority only *in usu*, that is the Word (= the Gospel) gives it authority and is the means for understanding it. The Reformation taught Christianity that "the knowledge of the Gospel can never be gained and maintained otherwise than critically." The Gospel itself produces the critical faculty which judges the Bible. The evangelical criterion is already in use in Paul's distinction between the *gramma* (Scripture isolated from the Spirit) and *pneuma* (Scripture understood with the Spirit, "the

2. "Hermeneutik," *Die Religion in der Geschichte und Gegenwart* (3. Aufl. Tübingen: J. C. B. Mohr, 1959), III, 256.
3. *History and Hermeneutic* (Philadelphia: Westminster Press, 1966), pp. 41–42.
4. "Vom theologischen Recht historisch-kritischer Exegese," *Zeitschrift für Theologie und Kirche*, 64 (1967): 259–281; cf. his 1962 paper "Thoughts on the Present Controversy about Scriptural Interpretation," *New Testament Questions of Today*, trans. W. J. Montague (Philadelphia: Fortress Press, 1969), pp. 260–285.

divine power which conveys the righteousness of faith and therefore stands in opposition to the law of the old Mosaic covenant"; cf. 2 Corinthians 3 and Rom. 2:29). The basis of historical criticism is Paul's understanding of justification and the Reformation's distinction of law and Gospel.

Käsemann supports his views with an historical argument about the formation of the canon. That history shows the Bible to be a human book with a very human history and appearance. The Gospel is what is important; therefore *sola scriptura* in the Reformation sense does not mean *tota scriptura*. When historical criticism points to problems in the history of the canon or within the Bible, it asks faith about the basis of its certainty and thereby fights against naive docetism in the understanding of the Bible. The tenacious hold of this docetism is demonstrated by the frequent ecclesiastical attempt to silence those who point out the problems by treating them as heretics.

If Käsemann fights against reactionary conservatism so strongly, he also rejects Bultmann's program of demythologization (and, by implication, all primarily existential interpretation). Although existential interpretation can plead not only Kierkegaard and the Englightenment, but also Luther (Commentary on Romans) as spiritual ancestors, its emphasis on understanding and decision shows its captivity to an individualistic understanding of the Gospel's work. It is elitist, for its synthesis of experience, hypothesis, and speculation fits only a small percentage of mankind. Historical criticism has shown that the Gospel is communal in outlook and belongs to wise man and fool alike. One's own understanding of reality dare not be the last norm for interpretation. Hermeneutics remains a science based on experience, not on principles. Therefore criticism must point out that existential interpretation frequently ends up as a nomism that is both tactless and loveless. (The position is close to Braaten.)

As usual Käsemann is interested in breaking contemporary idols. And criticism in line with the Reformation is the instrument to do so. For, "historical criticism must be content to lead us where men once questioned and doubted, believed and denied, as they heard the message of salvation. In that way it places us before decision and under promise."

Trutz Rendtorff justifies historical criticism with a different theological argument.[5] Historical criticism liberates the tendencies to freedom from authority and the criticism of tradition. These tendencies are part of the Protestant tradition and fitting for theology. Historical criticism is recognized by the church as the method for dealing with transmitted texts; but the method has limitations. It asks what *was* once Christian, and is the best method to discover the answer. But it is unconcerned with nonhistorical implications. Because it is critical and liberating, it points theology to the task of determining what is binding for today. Theology is directed to the contemporary world; it finds in historical criticism a good introductory science, a model of how men *once* understood the Christian faith. It receives the freedom to ask about the nature of Christianity.

These three positions share the viewpoint that critical theology is a positive instrument and almost indispensable. They differ from the older defense of historical criticism that was based primarily on the historical character of the Bible[6] or criticism's helpful results.[7] The mantle of the Reformation is cast over the Elisha of the historical critic. In the case of Ebeling the argument is somewhat of a tour de force, since its validity depends on the identification of Reformation criticism with existential interpretation. The *fides qua creditur* (faith as act of believing) swallows up the *fides quae creditur* (faith as content of belief). The law-Gospel distinction of the Reformation does not necessarily issue in *historical* criticism. Luther's canon criticism was of a different sort. Yet, the Reformation tradition is also not against historical criticism; however, it cannot be made a quasi-confessional method.

THE UNEASY TRUCE OF CONSERVATISM

Conservative theology has always found historical criticism a problem. On the one hand the conservative insists on the

5. "Historische Bibelwissenschaft und Theologie," *Theorie des Christentums* (Gütersloh: Gerd Mohn, 1972), pp. 41–60. Cf. Karl Lehmann, "Der hermeneutische Horizont der historisch-kritischen Exegese," *Einführung in die Methoden der biblischen Exegese*, ed. Josef Schreiner (Tyrolia: Echter Verlag, 1971), pp. 57–58.
6. Oscar Cullmann, "The Necessity and Function of Higher Criticism," *The Early Church*, ed. A. J. B. Higgins (Philadelphia: Westminster Press, 1956), pp. 3–20.
7. So Ernst Troeltsch; recently Günther Bornkamm, "Die ökumenische Bedeutung der historisch-kritischen Bibelwissenschaft," *Geschichte und Glaube* (München: Chr. Kaiser, 1971), II, 11–20.

importance of history for the Christian faith. On the other hand he fears the destruction which positivistic criticism brought. Therefore one strand of conservative theology tends to reject historical criticism out of hand as impious or to argue strongly against it.[8]

More and more conservatives, however, are making a truce with the method. G. Eldon Ladd, for example, argues with some vehemence that the helpful results of historical criticism should encourage conservatives to use the method, purifying it of its rationalist presuppositions with the conviction that the Bible "is the Word of God in the words of men."[9] The alternative to using historical criticism is an unthinking acceptance of tradition.

Friedrich Mildenburger demonstrates how a confessionally oriented Lutheran comes to terms with historical criticism.[10] His starting point is the conviction that the church's view of the Bible must be among the presuppositions for all biblical interpretation. The church holds (1) that the Bible is a unity and so its own best context for interpretation. This is the significance of the doctrine of inspiration and the formulation *scriptura sacra sui ipsius interpres* (Sacred Scripture is its own interpreter). The implication is that historical and theological interpretation must cohere. (2) The church also confesses that the Word of God and the Bible are inseparably joined by the Gospel as causative authority in the Bible. (3) The Bible is thus source and norm for the church (*Formula of Concord* of 1580); the Confessions are a guide to the reading of the Bible, for the Bible has a long history of interpretation. The interpreter stands in a tradition of interpretation and understanding of the Bible.

The Bible needs to be interpreted for the sake of the Gospel, says Mildenburger. Its subject is a history in which God is active. Historical criticism uses secular methods that place the

8. Erwin Reisner, "Hermeneutik und historischer Vernunft," *Zeitschrift für Theologie und Kirche*, 49 (1952): 223–238; Gerhard Bergmann, *Alarm um die Bibel* (4. Aufl. Gladbeck: Schriftmissionsverlag, 1965); Robert Preus, "Offenbarungsverständnis und historisch-kritische Methode," *Lutherischer Rundblick*, 11 (1963): 170–187; 12 (1964): 2–12.
9. *The New Testament and Criticism* (Grand Rapids: Wm. B. Eerdmans, 1967).
10. *Die halbe Wahrheit oder die ganze Schrift* (München: Chr. Kaiser Verlag, 1967). In *Theologie für die Zeit* (Stuttgart: Calwer Verlag, 1969) he evaluates the work of many key figures in the development of historical criticism.

Bible into general world history, give it a critical reading, and thus destroy its special character. Because its criterion is present knowledge, it excludes God from history and forms a unified picture of history without God. Modern biblical studies either ignore or strike a compromise in the conflict between the axioms of critical history and the dogmatic position of the church. Modern biblical studies use critical methods to hear in the canonical texts decisive material that can be heard nowhere else. Thus it seeks to avoid both fundamentalism and positivism.

This compromise is unavoidable, in Mildenburger's opinion, for both the church's position of faith and the historical tradition are present realities. The compromise allows the theologian to use the methods of philology and history, while respecting the unique character of the canon. If this compromise does not hold, then the conflict between church doctrine and historical method cannot be resolved. The Reformation principle makes critical reading of the Bible necessary, since some things in the Bible serve an intention other than the evangelical. But, argues Mildenburger, this is not criticism according to a historian's standard of truth, which the church cannot recognize. History has a legitimate function in showing the variety in the Bible and the unique character of each voice, no more.

Preserving the unique character of the Bible while recognizing the validity of the historian's claim is the basic problem not only of conservative Christians, but of all Christians. Ladd and Mildenburger demonstrate that a new evaluation of history is abroad in conservatism. Neither scholar is responding out of fear. The history of conservative American Protestantism shows that the only fruitful approach is to seek to combine theological convictions and historical methods. A rigid conservatism that reacts out of fear to banish scholars from the church by pushing them into the context of secular scholarship serves only to enshrine tradition in the place of the Scriptures. It also tends to remove scholarship from the community of the believing church—and that does more to radicalize it than does the use of historical criticism.

HISTORICAL CRITICISM UNDER ATTACK

In recent years two nontheologians have reacted to the methods in use by biblical scholars. In each case a significant critique from the standpoint of a nontheological discipline makes a contribution to the current discussion. The German historian August Nitschke evaluated exegetical methods and found them wanting because "biblical criticism . . . remains unhistorical in its procedures."[11] He examines the claim of Willi Marxsen that what is historically false in the Gospels may nevertheless be theologically significant.[12] An example would be the dating of the crucifixion in John to support Jesus as passover lamb (cf. 1 Cor. 5:7) or the placing of words on Jesus' mouth that he never said. The historian is nonplused by such fine distinctions, for the Gospels mean to give an historically reliable account. There are three conceivable reasons for changing the facts: (1) Explanation: An author living later or in a different culture changes facts to make what happened clear. (2) Illustration: Living in a mythological world he may change facts to give them a special symbolic content. The resulting strongly unified and closed picture makes the historian suspicious. (3) Contradiction: The author does not change events, but formulates a new doctrine on the basis of the events, e.g., ascribing to Jesus a messianic consciousness he did not claim. Numbers two and three are suspect, for two leads to unreliable facts and three is falsification.

Current exegetical method is strongly influenced by philological and sociological method. It seeks (1) to isolate the elements ascribed to Jesus in the tradition in order to excise them (a philological goal) and (2) to determine how the ideas that influenced the evangelists represent the thought, faith, or ideology of some group (a sociological goal). Historians use both techniques, but with a different goal. The historian asks whether the persons and events described in the text "really lived and are adequately represented." One does not resort to the philological or sociological concern until there is no longer a chance that the events described actually took place. The historian's method is his own. He "treasures the witnesses most who faithfully report what they have seen and heard even if it leads to contradictions." Nitschke illustrates this principle from Matt. 10:23 and 10:5, which stand out like erratic blocks in Matthew 10. A historian would here trust Matthew as a faithful chronicler, seek access to the person of Jesus from this

11. August Nitschke, "Historische Wissenschaft und Bibelkritik," *Evangelische Theologie*, 27 (1967): 225–236.
12. Willi Marxsen, *Der Streit um die Bibel* (Gladbeck: Schriftmissionverlag, 1965).

point of departure, and conclude that Jesus did raise a personal claim.

Nitschke concludes that the desire of biblical scholars to be as scientific and critical as possible has imprisoned them inside a method that is not adequate for its object, and so is unsatisfactory in its results. If the criteria of radically critical scholars are correct, these scholars cannot flee to the early church, whose opinions and narratives can have at best decorative, but not substantive function. As an historian Nitschke does not think the arguments convince. He is much more confident of the trustworthiness of the Synoptics and convinced as historian that Jesus regarded himself as messiah and coming judge, a claim which every believer must face.

Nitschke criticizes biblical scholarship for being too much influenced by literary-philological and sociological methods. Roland M. Frye, an American literary historian and critic, accuses contemporary Gospel criticism of being influenced too strongly by twentieth-century preconceptions and of failing to use good literary-historical canons.[13] It obscures or even denies the texts on the basis of *ex cathedra* presuppositions on the standard of "modern man," a standard that represents only a minority of people and is therefore a delusion.

Literary works should be dealt with on their own terms and allowed to establish themselves in their own way. For example, Bultmann's demythologization breaks the primary literary canon that "a literary work cannot be paraphrased." He seeks to turn myth into abstract idea. Yet myth communicates widely today, as the popularity of Milton and Dante shows. Myth should be brought under the theory of accommodation, an old theory which deserves to be revived. Myth is more effective than abstraction in literature. Criticism denies such valid insights.

Frye himself suggests that the Gospels are a form of dramatic history, a genre which has a message to communicate, which requires its audience to use imagination, and is selective of fact and time to achieve a representative condensation for a

13. "A Literary Perspective for the Criticism of the Gospels," *Jesus and Man's Hope* (Pittsburgh: Pittsburgh Theological Seminary, 1971): II, 193–221. In response to Paul Achtemeier's critique, "On the Historical-Critical Method in New Testament Studies; Apologia pro Vita Sua," *Perspective*, 11 (1970): 289–304, Frye restated his views in "On the Historical Critical Method in New Testament Studies: A Reply to Professor Achtemeier," *Perspective*, 14 (1973): 28–33.

general audience. To expect precision in such a work is to misunderstand it. Frye concludes with a rejection of form criticism, which he regards as a form of scholasticism that is without hard evidence, controls, and independent criteria. This "dismantling criticism" (which Frye later calls "erudite wheel-spinning") has largely been abandoned in English literary history. He also rejects positivistic historicism that treats history as "an unbroken succession of events in cause and effect relationships, within a purely naturalistic conception of possibilities." Such historicism, Frye holds, entails a reduction by rejection of whatever does not fit the *parti pris*; no amount of evidence, for example, will lead to an acceptance of the resurrection as a possibility within history. Such positivism violates literary canons, for the Gospels are not written on such a *propter hoc*, but on a *post hoc* view. They are thematic, not causal, in arrangement and metahistorical.[14]

Nitschke and Frye question the dominance of historical critical methodology as currently practiced. Nitschke reminds scholarship that history has a more restricted aim than is generally recognized. Their strictures suggest that biblical scholars would do well to separate historical and literary goals and techniques more carefully. In this way both sides of interpretation might better receive their due, and literary history might fructify biblical research.[15]

CRITICISM AND ESCHATOLOGY

The severest challenges to historical criticism have come from scholars schooled in the method. In recent years the systematician Wolfhart Pannenberg has attempted to bridge the gap between the results of historical criticism and the dogmatic statements of the church.[16] Two of his arguments are of signif-

14. Frye's conclusions were anticipated by Martin Franzmann, "The Hermeneutical Dilemma: Dualism in the Interpretation of Holy Scripture," *Concordia Theological Monthly*, 36 (1965): 502–533. Franzmann applies the category of poetry to some of the historical language in the Bible while also rejecting historicist assumptions.
15. Cf. R. Lapointe, *Les trois dimensions de l'hermeneutique* (Paris: J. Gabalda, 1967), pp. 75–76; Alex Stock, "Überlegungen zur Methode eines theologischen Kommentars," *Evangelisch-Katholischer Kommentar zum Neuen Testament, Vorarbeiten*, Heft 4 (Zürich, Einsiedeln, Köln: Benziger Verlag; Neukirchen: Neukirchener Verlag, 1973), pp. 11–55.
16. The essays are collected in *Basic Questions in Theology*, trans. George H. Kehm (Philadelphia: Fortress Press, 1970), vol. I: "The Crisis

icance here. Pannenberg accepts and affirms historical method as the legitimate mode of arriving at historical knowledge. But he tries to counteract its anthropocentric and imminentist bias. He contests the principle that analogy based on the universal homogeneity of all events can serve as a criterion of reality (pp. 48–49). Analogy, whose function is generally to stress the similar and disregard the particular, is a valuable means of advancing knowledge. But it can—and in biblical research should—be used with a recognition of its limitations. Theology, whose transcendent God is free of the cosmic order, is interested in the individual and the particular. Analogy should be used in theology to find the particular! That a reported event bursts analogies with otherwise real events is still no reason to dispute its factualism. Thus the resurrection cannot be rejected through the use of analogical reasoning (p. 49).[17]

In the second place, Pannenberg seeks to bridge the gap between history and theology by making universal history the subject matter of theology and the mode of divine revelation (p. 61). God is the Lord who breaks into history, as the whole of biblical witness testifies. One must learn from history how God works. But history can only be understood in its totality from its end, which is proleptically present in Jesus. In this way history becomes the mode of revelation, and so historical research must be able to demonstrate the dogmatic content of Scripture (p. 191).

Pannenberg thus seeks a midde course between history and the dogmatic tradition by calling positivist assumptions into question on the one hand and by elevating history to the central category of theology on the other. He has been criticized for undervaluing the revelatory character of the Word; history is held to be so clear by Pannenberg, according to Braaten, that the interpretive Word of the kerygma is no longer indispensable. The Word is swallowed up by the "facts" of history.

Jürgen Moltmann avoids that problem. He opposes both existential subjectivism and historical positivism in an important discussion of history as eschatology and the implications

of the Scripture Principle," pp. 1–14; "Redemptive Event and History," pp. 15–80; "Hermeneutic and Universal History," pp. 96–136; "On Historical and Theological Hermeneutic," pp. 137–181.

17. Pannenberg's arguments on analogy were recently discussed by Ted Peters, "The Use of Analogy in Historical Method," *Catholic Biblical Quarterly*, 35 (1973): 475–482.

this view has for historical criticism.[18] Against existential interpretation he points out that theological statements in the New Testament, e.g., "Jesus Christ is Lord," have both a specific content and a relationship to personal existence. Therefore the existential question cannot have a priority over the historical question, for it is legitimate to ask "What really happened?" An existential interpretation that does not have a corresponding reality in history is not helpful. The subjectivism of personal experience is nonhistorical and forces theology into an intellectual dualism of historical positivism and existential knowledge.

Moltmann characterizes historical positivism as that view of history which calls historical traditions true or false on the basis of the "closed causal chain" in historical events. Positivism holds that history is "controllable" from the sources, verifiable in principle, and capable of being grasped by a later age (pp. 62–63). It objectifies its object, and therefore assumes that the past is passé. It is the child of French and English positivism in the nineteenth century. It has no tie to the Reformation, no inner conceptual relationship to *sola fide*, and ignores Luther's attempt to free theology from scholastic metaphysics. Moltmann thus rejects the attempts to justify historical criticism confessionally.

History seeks events in relationship. The closed causal chain is *one* attempt to describe the relationship, but it does not have exclusive rights to the field. Its weakness, according to Moltmann, is demonstrated by its inability to admit that philosophy, art, or religion have a history that can be written. The closed chain of cause and effect limits and ossifies the material in advance through a dogmatic decision to seize only a part of the subject matter of history. The relationships in history cannot be determined in advance, however, but can be recognized only through an understanding of the subject matter treated and the events around which history moves (pp. 79–81).[19]

History is always a history of something in progress, open, unfinished, and still in the process of definition. History can be

18. "Exegese und Eschatologie der Geschichte," *Perspektiven der Theologie* (München: Chr. Kaiser Verlag, 1968), pp. 57–92.
19. Moltmann bases his description primarily on Ernst Troeltsch. One can question whether this decision does justice to the variety of historical method in either the nineteenth or the twentieth centuries. The modern German discussion is still dominated by the shadow of Troeltsch.

given meaning only from its end, even in terms of anthropology. Moltmann's basic position revises the understanding of history. History does not deal with the facts of a petrified past, but with an open-ended *fieri* (becoming), with *rebus sic fluentibus* (matters in flux). Christian revelation is like historical study in that it seeks to reveal how things really are, "*wie es eigentlich gewesen ist.*" It does not replace historical research, but demonstrates that history is the arena (*Spielplatz*) in which the effective Word of election, calling, justification, and commissioning does its work.[20] It is the Lord who makes the dead alive (Rom. 4:17), who is at work in history. History is not itself revelation (*pace* Pannenberg), but the field of the Lord's power, where God's eschatological lawsuit on behalf of the truth comes to its fullness. History moves toward an eschatological goal, proclaimed in the resurrection of Jesus. Thus memory becomes an exhortation to hope and the mode of hope. The closed causal chain of historicism can grasp what was and is, but is incapable of knowing where things are going. Only faith responding to the revelation of God in Christ can look to the goal. If historical criticism is to be fruitful, it should be used in the service of such eschatological hope.[21]

HISTORICAL CRITICISM AS METHODOLOGICAL CRISIS

Peter Stuhlmacher, a student of Ernst Käsemann's and his successor in the chair of New Testament at Tübingen, has launched a broadside against historical criticism in recent years.[22] But he does not stand alone. He represents a group of

20. Moltmann comes close to Hans Walter Wolff's formulation of the prophetic idea of history: "For the prophets, history is the goal-directed conversation of the Lord of the future with Israel." "The Understanding of History in the O.T. Prophets," *Essays on Old Testament Interpretation*, ed. Claus Westermann, trans. James Luther Mays (Richmond: John Knox Press, 1963), p. 338.

21. We should include a discussion of historical criticism in Roman Catholicism, but the literature has grown to such magnitude in recent years that it cannot be contained within the limits of this chapter. See the article by Karl Lehmann, above, note 5; Josef Ernst, ed., *Schriftauslegung* (München: Paderborn; Wien: Friedrich Schöningh, 1972); and Josef Blank, *Verändert Interpretation den Glauben?* (Freiburg: Herder, 1972).

22. "Neues Testament und Hermeneutik—Versuch einer Bestandaufnahme," *Zeitschrift für Theologie und Kirche*, 68 (1971): 121–161; "Thesen zur Methodologie gegenwärtiger Exegese," *Zeitschrift für die neutestamentliche Wissenschaft*, 63 (1972), 18–26; "Zur Methoden-und Sachproblematik einer interkonfessionellen Auslegung des Neuen Testaments," *Evangelisch-Katholischer Kommentar zum Neuen Testament. Vorarbeiten*, Heft 4 (Einsiedeln, Zürich, Köln: Benziger Verlag; Neukirchen: Neukirchener Verlag, 1973), pp. 11–55.

younger scholars,[23] for whom the defense of historical criticism no longer appears necessary, and whose problems appear to need discussion and solution, if biblical scholarship is not to stultify.

Stuhlmacher agrees that the historical critical method is, without argument, indispensable for theology ("Thesen," p. 19). Yet the *miserere*, the wretched state, of the discipline shows that exegesis has reached a crisis situation. There are mutually exclusive opinions on every topic or question in the discipline, a scandal in a scientific discipline. This Jeremiad concludes that exegesis "is caught in the lack of clarity about principles in her own method." The individual exegetical processes all raise questions ("Thesen," pp. 22–25; "Zur Methoden," pp. 22–45). But these questions are minimal in comparison to the problems raised by the understanding of the task and method of historical-critical exegesis. The discipline is in need of drastic self-correction.

Historical criticism is more than a mere set of techniques for the analysis of documents of a past age.[24] It is the child of the Enlightenment and historicism; it is still dominated by Troeltsch's principles (systematic criticism, analogy, and universal correlation). Historical criticism has led to a gap between historical and theological understanding, for it seeks to understand all historical materials by reason and expects to arrive at truth. Instead it remains captive to its own limited method and its notion of possibility in argumentation ("NT Herm.," pp. 130–131). In spite of its defenders' claims, it does not equal the theological criticism of Reformation theology (a point of view shared by Hahn, pp. 2–3, and supporting Moltmann).

Stuhlmacher argues that the contingency of the various "criticisms" should be recognized; often they are not historical

23. They would include Jürgen Moltmann; Ferdinand Hahn, "Probleme historischer Kritik," *Zeitschrift für die neutestamentliche Wissenschaft,* 63 (1972): 1–17; and Martin Hengel, "Historische Methoden und theologische Auslegung des Neuen Testaments," *Kerygma und Dogma,* 19 (1973): 85–90. Hengel's theses are both a summary of the problematics and a statement of positions.

24. Ulrich Wilckens, "Über die Bedeutung historischer Kritik in der modernen Bibelexegese," *Was heisst Auslegung der Heiligen Schrift?* (Regensburg: Friedrich Pustet, 1966), p. 133. A similar criticism is made by Lehmann, "Der hermeneutische Horizont," pp. 64 ff. He also criticizes ("Probleme," p. 45) Heinrich Zimmermann, *Neutestamentliche Methodenlehre. Darstellung der historisch-kritischen Methode* (4. Aufl. Stuttgart: Verlag Kath. Bibelwerk, 1974) for claiming to describe historical criticism, but never discussing it as a system.

enough in their approach (e.g., source and redaction criticism). But the broader field is occupied by an attack on the adequacy of the method for dealing with its object, the Bible. Historical criticism brings a concept of truth to the Bible that is not able to give full access to reality in history. It will either lead to "a conflict between theological intention and the tendentiousness of the method or introduce historical criticism into theological thought as a disturbing or destructive element" ("Zur Methoden," p. 46). We need a complete rethinking of the legitimacy, limitations, and need for development of historical criticism in contemporary exegesis.

Stuhlmacher makes significant contributions to the discussion of the theological framework and methodological presuppositions of historical criticism. He identifies two problem areas: (1) the lack of an integrating view of history and reality; (2) the failure to take into account the change in the understanding of tradition in New Testament studies. Both suggest that there is need to expand the field of New Testament labor ("NT Herm.," p. 144). Stuhlmacher proposes that this be done around two foci.

He offers the addition of a fourth principle to Troeltsch's three, to serve as the counter pendant to the historian's methodical doubt. He calls it the principle of perception (*das Vernehmen*), and defines it as "the readiness to take up and work through the claim (*Anspruch*) of the tradition, its posited truth, and its effectual history" ("NT Herm.," p. 148; "Zur Methoden," p. 48). He thus puts himself into basic disagreement with historical skepticism ("Thesen," pp. 23–24). Stuhlmacher sets this principle into the theological framework of the third article, i.e., interpretation must be done in such a way that faith becomes active in exegesis ("Thesen," p. 20). The interpreter must be ready "to allow in all seriousness the speech about God's action in Jesus Christ, i.e., the faith proclamation of the New Testament, as an essential truth for mankind."[25] Stuhlmacher is consciously going back to classical Lutheranism's formulation of the *testimonium spiritus sancti internum* (the internal witness of the Holy Spirit) and

---

25. "Zur Methoden," p. 42. In "NT Herm.," p. 149, Stuhlmacher refers to Georg Picht, "Theologie in der Krise der Wissenschaft," *Evangelische Kommentare*, 3 (1970): 199–203. Picht argues that one must understand the content and power of love, grace, sin, etc., if one is to discover the value and power of the biblical texts.